Ireland: Mythical, Magical, Mystical

A Guide to Hidden Ireland
The Hidden Gems Series

Christy Nicholas

Green Dragon Publishing

2024 Edition

Published by Green Dragon Publishing
Beacon Falls, CT
www.GreenDragonArtist.com

Table of Contents

Introduction

What comes to your mind when you hear the word 'Ireland?' Perhaps you envision fairies dancing around a mushroom circle in eerie starlight? Enormous pints of Guinness lined up on an antique wooden bar? Men with jaunty caps riding wooden carts pulled by tired donkeys?

Every person has a different impression, a different idea and ideal, when they think of a particular place. Ireland itself has such a varied past and present that the images conjured up are many-faceted, like a huge emerald, glinting bits of its life into each aspect of your mind and memory.

I've been to Ireland several times, and it holds a special place in my heart and in my head. Ireland is *m'anam an bhaile*, my soul's home, in Irish. It is a place I feel comforted, warm, and welcome. I wish to share some of this peace and serenity with others. Please, feel free to join me on my journey through Ireland, its history, mystery, and magic.

In this book, I will explore many aspects of Ireland. It possesses a rich mythical and historical culture, and a great part of this culture relates to the magic of the land and its people. There have been, and remain, many mystical parts of the island, but the people are what make Ireland what it is today. Of course, music is also an integral part of the culture. I will explore some stunning landscapes and architecture for the photo bugs and will then explore some of the practical aspects of travel in Ireland. I have listed some advice on ways to save money while on your journey and delved into some hidden places which most tourists pass by. In the back of the book, you will find several maps and resources to help with further research and information.

Please, enjoy your journey through my book. And, if I have convinced you to travel to this magical place, please let me know. I think everyone should visit Ireland and be enriched by its incredible sense of the mystical, magical, and mythical.

Torr Head, Antrim

The Mythical Facet—History and 'Myth'tery

Much of Irish history is shrouded in the mists of time and oral tradition. Most of what we know, or what we think we know, is classified as myth, as we have virtually no written evidence of the tales. The written sources we do have are sometimes unreliable as to historical accuracy and were most often transcribed from oral tradition by monks. These monks were probably torn between recording the local culture and discouraging belief in the pagan gods and traditions of this land. Therefore, they very likely colored the myths with Christian sensibility. Evidence exists suggesting many of the human legendary heroes were once worshiped as gods in their own right.

Historically, people arrived in Ireland between 10,500 and 8,000 BCE, shortly after the last miniature ice age covered the island in glaciers, though some recent evidence dates back to as long as 33,000 years ago. These Neolithic hunter-gatherers wandered the land, living off its bounty. Several waves of invaders came over the centuries, the final major one being the Celts from the Iberian Peninsula. Vikings and Normans came later, but the essential genetic makeup of the people of Ireland was already set.

In his book called *Saxons, Vikings, and Celts*, Bryan Sykes describes his work on the DNA of Ireland and the UK. He is a genetic archeologist, looking for clues of migration patterns in different areas of the British Isles and Ireland using genetic markers in today's population as compared to those of discovered skeletons in the areas, such as a 12,000-year-old skeleton in Cheddar, England. It was fascinating reading, and proved, genetically, Celts and Picts (the race in Scotland before the Gaels arrived) were the same race. As such, they likely had a common set of beliefs and language, back before the seas rose and cut the islands from each other. However, we shall leave Scotland for another book and concentrate on our Emerald Isle. So much for proven history, and on to the fun part.

Yeats Country, Sligo

There are several 'cycles,' sets of tales, about prehistoric Ireland:

- The Mythological Cycle (or Book of Invasions) tells tales of the various invasions of the land.
- The Ulster Cycle tells tales of heroic acts by kings and champions in Ulster and Connacht.
- The Fenian Cycle does the same for the folk of Leinster and Munster.
- The Historical Cycles are a bardic tradition of the history (or mythology) of the kings of Ireland.

While going into extensive detail about each cycle is beyond the scope of this book, I will delve into some of the more interesting points, so as to ground you in the essence of each.

THE MYTHOLOGICAL CYCLE

The Mythological Cycle is mostly comprised of a set of tales known as *Lebor Gabála Érenn*, the Book of Invasions or the Book of Conquests, and is, like the other tales of Ireland, filled with politics, battle, love, magic, and outrageous tales of feats of strength and revenge. It recounts, via myth and story, the invasions of the different peoples of Ireland over the course of its history. How closely these invasions are rooted in reality we may never know. However, once we reach the invasion of the sons of *Mil* (some time before 100 BCE), we start getting into territory which is corroborated by archeological evidence. These are the Celtic tribes who migrated from northern Spain. The earliest renditions of these tales seem to have come from the 8th to 11th century and are therefore heavily influenced by this later Christian ideal, but still manage to retain some of their pre-Christian magic.

Other parts of the Mythological Cycle are made up of the *Metrical Dindshenchas*, or Lore of Places, and other stand-alone tales such as The Dream of Aengus, the Wooing of Étaín, and The Tragedy of the Children of Lír.

If you want a delightful rendition of these tales, I highly recommend the Celtic Myth Podshow. Hosts Ruth and Gary Colcombe create many engaging dramatizations of these tales on their show and bring the stories to life.

But let us go back into the time before history, of land before remembering, and tales before writing. I have included a small list of names in their English versions and Irish versions in the appendix, for easier reading later on.

Go back… back into the mists of time, a time before writing, a time before people, a time before the island of Ireland had seen its first people… the mists start to rise,

showing the green, rolling hills, covered in trees, deer, and nothing more.

Poulnabrone Dolmen, Clare

Cessair

The tales tell of the first people to set foot in Ireland. Noah's granddaughter (yes, Noah of the Old Testament), Cessair, arrives on Ireland's emerald shores with one ship, forty-nine other women, and three men. Like chattel, the women are divided among them. Evidently, the Gods are not pleased by this. These groups were to populate the island, but a deluge comes along and washes away all but one man, *Fintán mac Bóchra*. Fintán lives for a further 5,500 years in several animal guises, shifting from one animal to another as each life is completed, gaining wisdom and stories. He becomes an honored *Seanchaí*, or storyteller, for Ireland, and this becomes an archetype in many tales.

Partholón

Three hundred years later, another descendent of Noah and Emzara settles in Ireland with his people and three sons, having come from Greece or Anatolia. They lived in peace and prosperity for ten years. However, they are then set upon by the evil *Fomóire*, a race of seafarers from Tory Island. While they win, they are then killed off by a mysterious sickness, and all die but one, *Tuan mac Cairill*. Tuan, like Fintán, spends many lives as different animals, and becomes a storyteller of great renown and wisdom. There is definitely a theme running here, explaining the wealth of tales and wisdom in the oral tradition. It also sets a tradition of honoring the elderly, those that have seen things in their life, and passed on that wisdom to the young. The Irish honor their elderly and wise, and invaders aren't very lucky, it seems.

The Quiet Man Bridge, Mayo

Neimheadh

The people of *Neimheadh*, or Nemed, a relative of Partholón, came to Ireland thirty years later. Once again, the Fomóire battled them. They win, but a subsequent sea battle floods Ireland and most of the Nemedians die. The few survivors are dispersed around the world. Don't worry, they come back.

Fomóire

The Fomóire (or Fomórians) were a magical race of beings thought to be semi-divine, roughly equivalent to the concept of chaos, such as the Titans in Greek mythology or the Frost Giants in Norse mythology. They were opposed to a later group of immigrants, the *Tuatha dé Danann,* and were part of many conflicts with them. They may represent the gods of the pre-Celtic people of Ireland, demonized for modern consumption.

Fir Bolg

250 years after the scattering of the Nemedians, some of the descendants return to Ireland, and are separated into three groups. The Fir Bolg, the *Fir Domnann*, and the *Gáilióin*. They are only in charge for thirty-seven years before the next invasion, perhaps the most famous one, that of the Tuatha dé Danann. They don't encounter the Fomóire. The Fir Bolg are also frequently demonized, as anyone who opposed the Fair Folk were in Irish stories. They are sometimes described as ugly, misshapen, and of evil countenance, gross caricatures of the beautiful Fair Folk. They were seen as unfair, warlike, devious, and greedy. It is thought that the name Fir Bolg came from 'Men of the Bag.'

Tuatha dé Danann

Yet another group of Nemedian descendants came from 'the far north.' Most stories described them as shining, beautiful, tall, and magical. The elves of Tolkien are thought to derive from the stories of this race.

Cork

They are skilled in magic and art, and they arrive giving battle to the Fir Bolg. They drive the tribe to the outer islands, but their king, *Nuada*, loses his hand in battle. Under Irish tradition, no man with a blemish can be king, so he retires, and the kingship is given to *Bres*, who is half-Fomóire.

Bres rules unfairly. He started extracting heavy taxes, and offering wretched hospitality, a high crime in Irish eyes. Nuada sees this and wants to help his people again. He asks his physician to fashion a shining silver hand to replace the one he lost when his hand was severed. Bres is forced to step down, and Nuada is once again king. However, the Fomóire still exact a crippling tax upon the Tuatha dé Danann, two-thirds of their annual harvest and cattle, so they are still an oppressed people.

Bres, in a huff of discontent, goes over to his father's people, the Fomóire, and asks for their help in taking back his kingship. His father realizes his son has been a poor ruler, saying he couldn't keep it by justice, he should therefore not take it by force. Instead, being the spoiled brat he is, Bres goes to king Balor of the Evil Eye, who has the power to kill with his gaze.

Balor raises his forces and invades the Tuatha lands. The battle goes back and forth between the two over many days, but finally Balor is killed by *Lugh* of the Long Arm, a nicknamed earned due to his exceptional skill with the spear. Lugh is a princeling who is Balor's own grandson and fulfilling a prophecy. He was raised away from his family, and taught all the skills of a king's court, to guard, sing, dance, sew, cook, etc. The prophecy said he would kill Balor, and he does. Lugh shoots a mighty slingshot at Balor, and, like David, defeats the giant foe. This is also quite reminiscent of Oedipus Rex, and the futility of trying to derail prophecy.

After this mighty battle, Tuatha dé Danann lived in peace (well, as much as the Irish ever lived in peace) for a hundred and fifty years.

Sons of *Míl*

In the north of Spain, a Celtic tribe is restless, looking for greener pastures. Their land is drying out, and crops are no longer lush enough to support them. A man named *Íth* sees

Ireland from atop a tower on a clear day and braves the rough seas to discover what he may see.

He discovers a land rich and green, filled with animals and arable land. He travels inland and comes in contact with the Tuatha dé Danann during a dispute on the Hill of Tara. He helps them solve a problem between the chieftains by convincing each they were fairly treated by the others. However, as part of this resolution, he waxes lyrical of the bounty of the land, and the locals fear he wants Ireland for himself, so they follow him back and attack him. He dies on the return to Iberia. His family, sons of his uncle, Míl, come back to Ireland to avenge his death.

Three sisters greeted them when they arrived. Each is lovely, tall, and elegant. Many religions have triple goddesses in their pantheon, and this is one of several in the Celtic myths. Each sister is a queen of Ireland, and they rule one year in three, as their husbands do as king. They are Banba, Fodla, and Ériu, and each demands their name be the name of the island. The poet of the Milesians, Amergin the Bard, promises each sister that this will be true if they are victorious.

The Milesians make an agreement with the Tuatha dé Danann; they are to get back in their ships and sail out into the ocean for a distance of nine waves. When they try to return, the Druids of the Tuatha conjure up mighty storms and mists so they cannot land. Each time the boat tries to get close to the shore, the wind, rain, and fog forces them back beyond the ninth wave.

The Milesians circle the island three times until, finally, Amergin dispels the storms with powerful poetry, called the Song of Amergin. This poem, or song, calms the waters, quiets the winds, and scatters the fog so the Milesians can finally land. The two armies do battle, and while the Tuatha dé Danann have magic, the Milesians have cold steel, something the Tuatha dé Danann cannot abide, so they are defeated.

Finally, an agreement is made between the two powerful races. The Tuatha dé Danann are given the world beneath the surface, giving rise to the legends of the *Sídhe*, the fairy folk, the Fae. To this day, one must not disturb a fairy mound, or risk the wrath of the Fair Folk beneath.

This is the point in the legends where history becomes part of the myth. We have started discovering archeological evidence, historical records, and at least some verification of the tales of the Irish after this point. Genetic evidence connects the Galician tribes of Spain with the pre-Norman Irish, and digs have found numerous belongings, trade goods and burial artifacts to corroborate this particular tale of migration.

Waterford

THE ULSTER CYCLE

This cycle of tales is also called the Ulaid Cycle, or the Red Branch Cycle, and has sagas of heroes in the eastern Ulster and northern Leinster regions. These are the tales to stir a man's blood to heroic acts, to fight off armies with one arm tied behind their back, to leap tall buildings with a single bound... well, perhaps not that. But they are stories that are told to emphasize the good and the bad in all men, that all acts of bravery and foolishness have consequences.

The main characters in these tales are King *Conchobar*, *Cú Chulainn*, *Deirdre*, and Queen *Medb*. The events supposedly took place in the first half of the first century CE, though there is some evidence that parts of the tales occurred later.

The most famous of the tales is the *Táin Bó Cúailnge*, translated as the Cattle Raid of Cooley. And, while the Mythological Cycle was almost entirely populated by supernatural beings, there is only the occasional peppering of divine or semi-divine players in this cycle, perhaps a holdover of the ancient gods, or honoring of the Tuatha dé Danann.

The tales talk of the births of heroes, wooings and elopements, legendary feasts, bitter rivalries and battles, cattle raids, and of course, deaths.

At this time in Ireland, there was no high king. The country was divided into major areas: Munster in the south, Connacht in the west, Ulster in the north, Leinster in the east, and Meath in the center.

Sometimes one person was king over an entire region, but more often, it was made up of multiple, smaller kingdoms and fiefs. Seldom was there peace, as minor warlords and kings were constantly fighting to gain power and resources.

A king's dearest advisor was his druid, who went through decades of training to memorize the oral traditions of history, Brehon law, music, and the magic of the trees. Some scholars see these tales as purely imaginary, while others see them as mostly historical. We may never know how much truth there is to them. I prefer to believe these tales merely reflected the romance and heroics of the age.

King Conchobar

King Conchobar ruled Ulster from *Emain Macha*. This was a fortress on a hill, or a dun, near modern Armagh, and now known as Navan Fort. It was a center for government and magic through much of this age, a place where people met, came for justice, and worshiped the gods.

The name means Twins of Macha. There is a tale of Macha giving birth to twins, and she's the goddess of war, fertility, and horses. She was one of the aspects of the Morrigan, another triple goddess in the pantheon.

Conchobar's mother manipulated many people with adultery, bribery, and trickery to make her son king.

Usually, in tales such as the Greek and Roman myths, such underhanded means of gaining power are paid back in kind. However, in Irish myth, this was not always the case.

She secured a temporary kingship for her son, but once he was crowned, he was wise and fair enough that the people kept him, and the old king fled.

Conchobar was also well known for having many wives and many lovers and reserving the right to bed brides on their wedding night. This may be where the concept of *Primae Noctis,* or First Night, the right of a lord to take a bride on her wedding night, becomes popular in Celtic culture, though despite the movie, Braveheart, this was never a true policy.

Uragh Stone Circle, Kerry

Cú Chulainn

Cú Chulainn was a hero of semi-divine birth, the son of *Deichtine* (daughter of Conchobar mac Nessa, King of Ulster) and Lugh, the Shining One, the Sun God of Irish Myth.

His name was originally *Sétanta*, but after he killed a hound owned by the blacksmith, *Culann*, in self-defense, he vowed to guard the smith in place of the hound until a new one can be raised. *Cú* is the Irish word for hound, so he was thereafter known as Cú Chulainn, the Hound of Culann.

There are many wondrous tales of Cú Chulainn, tales of heroism and foolishness, tales of battle and lust.

He was Ireland's premier hero, the hero against whom all deeds were measured, and all bravery was compared. He was often shown as an Irish version of the Greek hero, Achilles, and his berserker rage could have been the inspiration for the Hulk stories (Stan Lee once said so).

The Causeway Coast

As a young man, Cú Chulainn trained with *Scáthach*, a warrior woman who lived on the Isle of Skye in Scotland, and who ran a fighting school. He fathered a son with the warrior woman, Aoife, while he was on the island.

This son was named *Connla* and was featured in other stories in this cycle. Cú Chulainn also learned the art of berserker rage, which led to loads of trouble and heartache throughout his stories. He had a magical spear from Scáthach, the *gea bolg*, which won many battles for him, but which was also the instrument of his death. More about Cú Chulainn later, though.

Deirdre of the Sorrows

This famous Irish romance recounts the tale of Deirdre, whose name means 'broken-hearted and sorrowful,' and the Sons of *Uisneach*. Uisneach is the geographical center of Ireland, and a sacred place of kings.

When Deirdre was born, the Druid foretold she would be the fairest woman in the land but would bring great sorrow if she married a king. Deirdre was described as 'dark of hair, white of skin, and red of lips.' For her protection, she was brought up in a fort, apart from all men but Conchobar and her foster father. Conchobar had his eye on her from the moment the Druid foretold her great beauty.

However, as was typical of such a situation, she didn't want to marry him, and dreamt of a younger husband. She told her nurse of her dreams and described her imagined love of raven hair and young heart. The nurse told her the man of her dreams was *Noísi*, one of the Sons of Uisneach.

He was a cousin to Cú Chulainn and a warrior of the Red Branch. Deirdre decided she must have this young man and put a *geis* (spell) upon him. He, of course, fell in love with her and, with the help of his two brothers, he stole her away. They traveled all over the land, evading capture by the enraged Conchobar. Eventually, they escaped to Scotland and got married.

The king of the Picts in Scotland was jealous of this great beauty, and wanted Deirdre for himself, so off they went again. Conchobar sent a message to Deirdre and Noísi, saying he was offering peace, and they believed him. Naturally, they were met by treachery, as most of these tales do, and Deirdre was brought to the king, while the brothers were killed.

Others heard of this terrible treachery and attack, and many men on both sides died, rendering the prophecy true, despite all the attempts to circumvent it. Deirdre lamented the loss of her love and wasted away for a year; she then took her own life, ending a tragic tale of love, betrayal, and hopelessness.

Queen Medb (Maev)

Queen Maev was a wonderful character in Irish myth; a strong woman who had power in her own right. While she made many poor decisions and ruled with pride and rage, she was a far cry from the meek, submissive females in many other mythologies.

Maev ruled Connacht with her husband, *Ailill mac Mata.* She was a very strong-willed queen, fiery and demanding. She wanted to rule equally, and when her first husband Conchobar refused, she left him and went to Connacht.

Dunseverick, Antrim

She was often understood to be a patron goddess of the land of Ireland. She frequently took lovers to her bed. Some may be familiar with Shakespeare's homage to her, as Queen Mab, in his immortal play, *Romeo and Juliet.* Like Cú Chulainn, there are many tales of this strong woman.

Táin Bó Cúailnge, or the Cattle Raid of Cooley

This tale is full of boasting and pride, and the downfalls of such sins. King Ailill boasted to his wife, Queen Maev, that his white bull was the best bull in all of Ireland. Maev was therefore goaded into finding a better one, to compete. She found a brown bull which belonged to an Ulster chieftain, *Dara mac Fachtna*. However, Dara was unwilling to sell or rent the bull, so Maev decided she had to steal it.

As her army approached Ulster, the opposing warriors of the Red Branch suffered from a curse of weakness (previously put upon them by Macha). That is, everyone except Cú Chulainn (remember him?) Our erstwhile hero raided and used guerilla tactics to slow the army before it arrived, which demoralized the opposing forces greatly. Finally, he agreed to meet, champion against champion, with his former teacher, Fergus, who was in command of Queen Maev's army.

The two heroes fought a mighty duel, day after day, matched equally in strength and prowess. Each night they slept and dreamt, only to wake and fight again.

After several days of duels, Cú Chulainn met the war goddess, the Morrigan, who was disguised as a young woman. He refused her sexual advances, so she harried and wounded him during his duels. His father, Lugh, sickened by this inequality, agreed to take his place in the duels until his son is healed.

Maev's raid was eventually a success. However, while the warriors of the Red Branch were still suffering from their curse, their sons picked up arms, but were slaughtered by Maev's army. This threw Cú Chulainn into a berserker frenzy and he killed seventy warriors.

When Maev finally brought the Brown Bull to Connacht, it fought the White Bull, and they both die.

The moral? Greed and pride are sins, punishable by loss and humiliation, and those who fight with honor and show kindness can win in the end.

The Ulster Cycle is full of heroism, treachery, love, and death. It seems to be too much drama to be contained within one lifetime, and perhaps it is simply a conglomeration of tales throughout Irish history, attached to known characters to make the tales more interesting.

They do, however, nicely sum up the culture of the pre-Christian Irish; warlike, proud, headstrong, and passionate. It also emphasizes that the wealth of the people lies in their cattle and their battle prowess, and that these tales are passed back and forth like a mug of ale.

THE FENIAN CYCLE

Also known as the Ossianic Cycle, this set of tales centers on the hero *Fionn mac Cumhaill* (Finn MacCool) and his warriors in a band called the Fianna. They were formed by *Cormac mac Airt*, then High King of Ireland, to protect the kingdom.

They fought off invaders in the summer and enjoyed the hospitality of those they protect in the winter. Some of the tales dealt with the excesses of this enjoyment, and the follies that derived from those excesses.

Because he was so young and unwise, the men didn't want to be led by Finn, so the young man went to find an education. Finn was studying with a poet, and accidentally touched the roasting Salmon of Knowledge, despite the poet's instructions not to touch it. When his finger was burned, he put it in his mouth, thus he tasted the salmon and received all its wisdom (in a similar tale, Merlin, or *Myrddin*, of Wales, does the same thing).

Finn was then admitted into the court of the High King at Tara and became the leader of the Clan Bascna. Using a magical harp which rendered all helpless, he killed a creature which terrorized the court every Samhain. As a result, he was made leader of the Fianna.

He married a woman, *Sadhbh*, who had been under a spell in the guise of a fawn. She was human when in his house at the Dun of Allen, but she was tempted out one day, turned into a fawn and bounds away among the hills of Ireland.

Despite all their searching, they never found her, but they did find a boy who had been raised by a fawn, named *Oisín*. They believed this boy to be Sadhbh's son. Oisín became a legendary bard and was the narrator of the tales of this cycle.

THE HISTORICAL CYCLE

These tales are also called the Cycles of the Kings, and, logically enough, contain tales of the kings of Ireland, such as Cormac mac Airt, *Niall* of the Nine Hostages, *Conn* of the Hundred Battles, and *Brian Bóruma mac Cennétig* (Brian Boru of Kennedy).

These tales would have been created and memorized by the Druids and handed down for teaching the folk of Ireland. The Druids did not write tales down but recited them in great feats of memory.

These kings ranged from mainly mythological kings, such as *Labraid Loingsech* (around 430 BCE) to Brian Boru, who was entirely historical (around 980 CE). Many of the tales were written down only in Christian times, and thus have been colored with Christian tints to make them more palatable to the monks. This is true of all the cycles, and we may never know what the original tales were like.

A most popular tale is of *Suidhne* (Sweeney), a pagan king who was awakened one morning by a bell. Searching for this rude interruption of his slumber, he found a newly built church. In a rage, he broke the bell, which angered the church fathers, who put a curse on him. He went insane and became like a bird, flitting about, and eventually died a broken man, ironically, under the care of a kind churchman. This tale may be one of many inspirations for the Lancelot tales in the King Arthur stories.

RECORDED HISTORY

After the Mythological Cycles above, we encounter mostly verifiable recorded history during the Age of Saints, roughly the 5th century CE forward. The Christian monks may have corrupted the pagan tales with their own view, but at least they wrote many of them down, and continued to keep track of the activities on this island up to, and including, the present day.

Ballynoe, County Down

While the scope of this book does not include an in-depth treatise on recorded history in Ireland, I believe that, in order to get the most out of your travels in Ireland, you should have at least a basic understanding of the major events and their effects upon the land and culture. Here are some of the salient events, and a brief description, in timeline form. I've also included some earlier events that have historical evidence to help anchor them in the mists of prehistory. The waves of different cultures in the early periods could correspond loosely to the Mythological Cycle tales.

- 8,000 BCE—The first Mesolithic hunter-gatherers arrived in Ireland, perhaps over a land bridge.
- 6,000 BCE—Neolithic culture rose, with megalithic tombs being built and standing stones being raised.
- 2,000 BCE—Bronze Age culture rose, heralding gold and bronze ornamentation, weapons and tools. This wave may represent the arrival of the Tuatha dé Danann.
- 600 BCE—Iron Age culture arrived with a gradual immigration of Celtic-speaking people into Ireland. The societal structure resembled that of other Celtic tribes in mainland Europe and the other Isles, including Druids and tribal kings. This last wave may represent the arrival of the Sons of Míl from Spain.
- 0 CE—Ulster Cycle tales are traditionally set at this time.

The Burren, Clare

- 3rd century CE—Fenian Cycle tales are traditionally set at this time.

- Early 5th century CE—Establishment of (and battle between) many of the ruling dynasties of Ireland, including the Uí Néill, Dal Cais, and Eóghanachta, which held power over much of the land for centuries.
- 432 CE—St. Patrick returned to Ireland to start converting the kings, and by proxy, the people, to Christianity. There had been earlier missionaries, but Patrick was the most remembered.
- 6th century—This was the Age of Saints and Scholars, and was a time of peace, prosperity and learning around the land. Monastic sites spring up around the country, including those founded by St. Columba and St. Brendan.
- 795 CE—The first Viking raids occurred in Ireland. At this point, they're mostly raids on the coastal settlements and up rivers, such as the River Liffey. The Vikings had bases in the Scottish Isles and the Isle of Man to conduct these raids.
- 852 CE—Vikings established a fortress at Dublin (Dubh Linn, meaning Black Pool). Ironically, the Vikings began assimilating into the Irish culture.
- 1014 CE—Battle at Clontarf, in which Brian Boru defeats Máel Mórda mac Murchada, which marked the beginning of the decline of Viking power in Ireland. Several settlements, such as Wexford, Waterford, and Dublin, were established by the Vikings. They continued to intermarry into Irish families.
- 1171 CE—Having been asked several times for help against a rival by Diarmait Mac Murchada, Henry II of England landed his forces at Waterford, signaling the beginning of the Anglo-Norman influence and power in Ireland. Richard 'Strongbow' de Clare, Earl of Pembroke, and the barons of the Welsh Marches came and married Diarmait's daughter, Aoife.
- 15th and 16th centuries—Various rebellions against Anglo-Norman/English power rose, with varying levels of success due to Irish patriotism and English apathy.

- 1540s—Dissolution of the Monasteries/Reformation—Due to the power of the Act of Supremacy, Henry VIII was given the authority over the churches in England and Wales, and he used this power to disband monasteries and abbeys, as well as smaller churches and friaries. He then appropriated their lands and incomes for his own use. While in Ireland, he technically only had power over the area known as the Pale (immediate area around Dublin), he passed legislation into the Irish Parliament to allow the dissolution to the rest of the island. This dissolution had a limited effect, as local landowners tended to help the local churches from complete dissolution.
-

- 17th century—Penal laws were created in order to keep the Irish Catholics under control and to accept the Anglican Church, and to ensure that only those of the Anglican Church wielded any power in the government or communities. These laws barred the Irish (Catholics) from holding land, serving in the army, taking office, speaking the native language, or marrying. Catholics had to pay a fee for missing Anglican Church services, and while tacitly tolerated, Catholic services must be held in private. Later they were outlawed, and the priests arrested when discovered.

- 1607 CE—The Flight of the Earls—the last Irish Earls with any power fled Ireland, ceding the power to the English.
- 1649 to 1650 CE—Cromwell led an invasion of Ireland to subjugate the island. As a Puritan, he was extremely hostile to the Catholic population, and the campaign was famously cruel and ruthless, with massacres, religious persecution, and burnt towns. The memory of this time and his activities are still strong in Irish minds.
- 18th century—More rebellions, failing penal laws and the English breaking agreements.

Glenariff Forest, County Antrim

- 1798 CE—Irish Rebellion of 1798, or the United Irishmen Rebellion. Inspired by the success of the American Revolutionary War, liberal Anglicans sought common cause with the oppressed Catholic populace to get reform and autonomy from the British government. One of the leaders, Wolfe Tone, traveled to the US and France to elicit assistance. The violence was in concentrated outbreaks, and resulted in many deaths and atrocities, and resulted in stricter oppression.

- 1801 CE—Acts of Union 1900 passed—the Kingdom of Ireland was now part of the United Kingdom of Great Britain and Ireland.
- 1829 CE—Catholics were now permitted to sit in Parliament.
- 1845-1851 CE—The Great Hunger (An Gorta Mór)—two-thirds of the potato crop was destroyed by a blight that turns the potatoes into black sludge, earning the nickname of Black '47 for the third year of the blight. Since the introduction of the potato around 1570 by Sir Walter Raleigh, the English had changed much of the crops over to potato farming, and now Ireland was almost entirely dependent on it. If the English hadn't taken most of the viable crops from the country, it wouldn't have been nearly as disastrous. The blight led to an estimated 1 million dead and 1 million emigrated.
- 

- 1916 CE—Easter Rising, aka Easter Rebellion—This was the most successful push for independence from England since the 1798 Rebellion. The Irish seized key government buildings in Dublin, such as the General Post Office, which became the rebel headquarters. While the Rising only lasted

7 days, the execution of its leaders rallied the Irish to the cause.

- 1919 CE—Declaration of Independence was issued.
- 1921- 1922 CE—Irish Civil War, aka Irish War for Independence—A treaty (Irish Free State) was signed with Great Britain, abolishing the Irish Republic of 1919, and making the state part of the British Commonwealth. Michael Collins (Pro-Treaty) and Éamon de Valera (Anti-Treaty) and their followers fought to establish the new form of the Irish state. The Pro-Treaty group won. This was when Northern Ireland was established as a separate state.
- 1937 CE—The new state of Ireland replaced the Irish Free State, though it was not formally declared a Republic until 1949. The Irish Constitution was written.
- 1969 CE—The Battle of Bogside—The beginning of 'The Troubles'; troops deployed in the streets in Northern Ireland. Riots, violence, assassinations, and other religious unrest lasted until the Good Friday Agreement, signed 10 April 1998. While there are still some people, unfortunately, who believe violence is still the answer, most activists have moved onto the political stage for the rest of the fight for independence for Northern Ireland.
- 1990 CE—Mary Robinson became the first female President of Ireland.
- 1995—2008 CE—Celtic Tiger period of great economic growth.
- 2007 CE—Celtic Tiger ends with housing bubble burst, bank scandal, and governmental power shift.
- 2020 CE – The housing crisis returned with a vengeance.

While I mention just one famine in Ireland, and only a couple of rebellions, there were many of both throughout the centuries, as well as plague, internal strife, and other major events. Irish history is one of struggle, conflict, but most of all, survival.

While much of this is due to outsiders trying to control the Irish people (Vikings, Normans, and English), much of it is also due to internal conflict and bickering among the tribes. The Celts as a whole were never a race that got along great with their neighboring Celts. Warfare has a long and honored tradition in the tribes, and the Irish epitomize that ideal even unto the present. Despite that, the Irish never invaded anyone else.

Summary

So, what does this all mean to the traveling tourist? It means the landscape of Ireland, both above and below, whether mist-covered hill or rocky mountain, is steeped in historical and mythical significance. Practically every square meter of this tiny country has something which occurred here; something which made the place special.

You can easily form a travel plan to visit, for instance, five stone circles in one day, or ancient forts, or burial mounds. You could travel to royal ancient Ireland, such as the Hill of *Uisneach*, the Hill of Tara, Maev's Tomb, the *Grianán Ailigh*. You could go from battle site to battle site, and never run out of places to visit. You could hop from fairy hill to fairy tree to fairy ring. Be creative, and find the hidden places, the spots which resonate in your very soul, and the ones which speak to your essence, and enjoy those spots. Do you find peace watching a waterfall, or a sunset over a sea cliff? Perhaps you love seeing the rolling green patchwork of farms, or the endless stone walls on the Aran Islands. Each aspect of this land is brimming with a past which brings more meaning to what you see. This is the Ireland we keep in our heart and our soul.

The Magical Facet—The Fair Folk

Glengesh Pass, Donegal

Everyone has heard of fairies, of creatures with supernatural powers to curse, to bless, to find gold, or to cause mischief. Literature and art are full of them, from Shakespeare to contemporary artists Amy Brown or Jasmine Beckett-Griffith. Western culture, especially in the US, is bred on Disney's Tinker Bell, children's books of flower fairies from Victorian artists, and grim tales of the darker side of these Fae folk.

In Ireland, fairies, known as the Sídhe (pronounced shee) or the Good Folk, originate from the Tuatha dé Danann, the people who immigrated to the island before the Sons of Míl. Supposedly full of powers, the Tuatha dé Danann could not bear to be near iron, and therefore their superior skills were for naught. Rather than leave the land they loved, they agreed to reside below the earth. For this reason, caves are said to be entrances into their underworld homes. Traces of this legend can be seen in the classic film, Darby O'Gill and the Little People, where Darby is led under a mountain to the Fairy King's palace. Ireland has countless portals, be they hills, hawthorn trees, caves, wells, or other sacred places.

A more Christianized origin of these creatures claims they are angels which fell to Earth before humans resided there. They live beneath the waves or gardens, and while some are evil, others can be helpful, as long as they are treated with respect.

While many modern legends show fairies to be sweet, kind, magical creatures, this is really a Victorian creation. The traditional views in Ireland and Scotland show the Sídhe to be mischievous to the point of cruelty—a force to be reckoned with. They are not sought out by the wise. In fact, most of the herb and spell lore of an almost forgotten era is meant to instruct how to keep you from coming to the Folks' attention.

Copper Coast

There are several types of fairies in Irish lore:

- The *Dullahan* is a dark, headless horseman who calls for the dead. He may be the origin of the Headless Horseman legends. There are also related legends of the Dark Hunt, which collects the dead on dark and stormy nights.
- The *Púca* (Pookha) is greatly feared in Ireland. He can take many forms, but often a sleek, dark horse with yellow eyes, scattering livestock and trampling crops. Livestock which won't produce eggs or milk are thought to have been terrorized by the Púca.
- Changelings are sickly fairy children who have been exchanged for healthy human children. This creature creates havoc and drains all the good luck from a family, and usually dies quickly. Sometimes these children are disguised older fairies, or enchanted blocks of wood, but their true nature eventually becomes evident. A bit of iron on the baby's clothes or in the crib is thought to prevent the human baby from being stolen.
- The *Grogoch* are half human, half-fairy creatures covered in hair with bad hygiene. They live wild and may help with planting or chores for a jug of cream and have great fear of the clergy.
- The *Bean Sídhe* (Banshee or fairy woman) is a spirit who screeches when someone is about to die, someone usually associated with a particular family. She can be seen as a hag or an older woman washing by the river. Often the stream will be red with the blood of the dying or dead. Some families claim to have their own Banshee who follows them from generation to generation.
- *Leipreachåns* (Leprechauns) are perhaps the best known of the Irish fairies. They are small men who make shoes and drink *poitín* (Potcheen, Irish moonshine). They have treasure and will only reveal it if tricked. This legend has been twisted and told so many times in modern culture, it's difficult to find what the traditional legend may have been. The *Cluricaun*

is a related creature, though more sinister. It steals, borrows, or sickens livestock and crops, and generally creates mayhem wherever it goes.

- The *Murúch* (Merrow) is a mermaid or merman, extremely beautiful, tempting, and not very friendly to humans. Some are selkies, who appear as seals unless someone steals their sealskin cloak, trapping them in human form. These selkies are said to be excellent mothers and wives but will quickly return to the sea if she finds her cloak, leaving her children on the land without a second thought. Sometimes there is a time limit to their human form. Seven years is a common time in tales.

While most modern Irish will laugh at you when you ask them if they believe in the Sídhe, or the Fae Folk, they will, nonetheless, refuse to do something they know to anger these 'nonexistent' creatures. As an example, there was a highway project to build a road in County Clare in 1999. The path of the road was to go through an area in which grew a lone hawthorn tree. No Irishman would dig up this tree, and eventually, the government was forced to divert the highway away from the tree to preserve it.

When I was in Ardara in County Donegal, drinking a pint of cider and chatting with the pub owner and her son, who was old enough (barely) to be tending bar, I mentioned this story. The son had no idea of the significance of the hawthorn tree as an entrance to the world of the Sídhe, but his mother was adamant about it. 'Have I taught you nothing? You never want to disturb a lone hawthorn tree!'

Fairy superstitions and beliefs:

- They are easily offended. Evidently, you shouldn't call them 'fairies' out loud, as they hate this name. The Wee Folk, the Sídhe, the Fair Folk, The Other Crowd, or even Them, are all preferable names.
- It is said the Last Harper (bard) of Ireland, Turlough O'Carolan, fell asleep on a fairy mound, and received the gift of fairy music.
- Hawthorn trees, unusual hills, rings of mushrooms, some glades, forts, and lone trees are sacred. Disturb them or fall asleep near them at your peril.
- Never build your house on a fairy path. Set four posts at the corner of the site overnight. If they are still there the next morning, you should be safe.
- If you offend a fairy, you may be hit by a Fairy Dart. This causes severe swelling in the hands or feet. The cure is an ointment made from unsalted butter and herbs, and the extraction of the dart. Splinters are often seen as Fairy Darts.
- Do not refuse a fairy what they ask. The rest of them will demand retribution, and your family may be cursed for generations.
- A pair of shovels across the mouth of a grave keeps out fairies. This is still seen today.
- Sometimes humans are brought to the fairy palace. Often, they return to the human world, only to long to go back. Sometimes they die in the longing.
- If you do go to a fairy palace or land, and you wish to return

home, eat or drink nothing, or you will be stuck there.

Many ancient tales of the fairies were collected by Lady Francesca Speranza Wilde (Oscar Wilde's mother) in 1887. Also, there are many tales by William Butler Yeats.

Doolin, Clare

I greatly enjoyed the book, The Red-Haired Girl from the Bog, a Landscape of Celtic Myth and Spirit, by Patricia Monaghan, as she delves into some fairy experiences she had on her travels. She writes of the mysticism in the land, and the ability of every person to discover it for themselves.

In your travels, be sure to honor the Fair Folk, even if you don't truly believe in them. It never hurts to be safe, right? It is best to keep an open mind on the subject of the Otherworld. Don't walk through the fairy rings of mushrooms on a green plain. Don't mess with the lone hawthorn tree. And don't dare fall asleep in a stone circle! If you feel a need to appease the Sídhe, leave out an offering for them; a bit of fruit, some milk, a lovely stone or a flower. If you've lost something, they may be persuaded to return it, if given sufficient gifts. Being respectful is important for people of all sorts, whether above the ground or below it.

Keep in mind that these beliefs are part of a living tradition. They aren't just cutesy things to play around with, they are a native religion. Please, treat the legends with respect. Should you be curious, a great resource on this living tradition is Lora O'Brien, a native teacher in Irish spirituality at Irish Pagan School.

The Mystical Facet—Gods and Saints

Valentia Island, Kerry

Ireland was a pagan land before the 5th century and a mostly Christian land after this time. Throughout this period, miracles, mystical battles, gods, and saints saturated the land and history with spiritual magic. The ground itself seems spiritual as you walk along its emerald slopes, soaking in centuries of curses and blessings, belief, and power.

I shall not make any judgment as to whether the pagan beliefs or the Christian beliefs are more correct. Proselytizing is not the purpose of this book. This is up to each individual to decide. I shall present the myriad aspects of the land and allow the reader to take what wisdom and interest they wish from them.

GODS

The Celtic pantheon is rather nebulous, as many tribes held their own beliefs. The Irish Celts were no different, but there are particular gods who were more commonly accepted. Most of them began as mythical or historical characters in the sagas of the Mythological Cycle, part of either the Fir Bolg or the Tuatha dé Danann and morphed into gods over the ages of oral tradition. They assigned aspects of Nature to the Divine and gave personality to many aspects of Nature.

The Annals of the Four Masters had this passage:

'Laeghaire *took oaths by the sun, and the wind, and all the elements, to the Leinster men, he would never come against them, after setting him at liberty.'*

The version in the *Leabhar na h-Uidhri* says:

'Laeghaire swore by the sun and moon, the water and the air, day and night, sea and land, he would never again, during life, demand the Borumean tribute of the Leinster men.'

Glenichaquin Park, Kerry

Cromm Crúaich—also known as Crom, Crom Cruach, Cen Cruach, the bleeding head, or the Crooked One of the Mound. He is known as the great Creator, the head of all gods. However, he does not have a very fatherly aspect, and is greatly feared. Perhaps he is more akin to the Greek concept of Chaos, the entity of void before order was created and imposed upon the universe. A common representation of Crom is a golden figure surrounded by twelve stone figures, perhaps other gods. St. Patrick was said to have destroyed the stone images with a sledgehammer.

An old reference to Crom has been recorded in Ogham letters (ancient Druidic writing), thus translated, *'In it Cruach was and twelve idols of stone around him, and himself of gold.'* In the old book Dinseanchus, we read thus of Crom: *'To whom they sacrificed the first-born of every offspring, and the first-born of their children.'* He is definitely associated with human sacrifice, in exchange for good crops and milk from cows.

Danu—Danu is the mother goddess. The Tuatha dé Danann are, literally translated, the children of Danu. She is a mysterious figure and does not appear as an active figure in the tales of adventure and war, as many others were. She is simply the mother of all. Her name is reflected in the Dan River in Russia and the Danube which passes through or touches the borders of ten countries, primarily in Romania. The Irish might have believed she was the creator of the Earth, and rivers of life flowed from her womb. Her breasts were the mountains. There are, in fact, a couple of mountains in County Kerry called 'the Paps of Danu'.

The *Dagda*—He is known as the Good God, the fatherly aspect of the divine pantheon. While Crom was more of a shadowy figure, the Dagda was very real and present in the tales of the Tuatha dé Danann. His feats of strength, diplomacy, and eating were legendary. Some say he was the son of Danu, while others say he was her father or husband. He is the protector of the Irish tribes, and well-loved. He wields a great club which could kill nine men at once, but the other end could bring life back to the dead or injured. He also has a magical cauldron, which is ever full of food. He has a magical harp which gave order to the seasons. He is associated with two pigs, one ever-growing and the other ever-roasting, the fruitfulness of the land, and justice for the people of Ireland.

Unlike most Irish gods, the Dagda is often portrayed with very human characteristics; oafish, crude, and sometimes comical. Despite this, he was High King after Nuada of the Silver Arm was injured in battle and led the Tuatha dé Danann in battle against the Fomóire.

Tullynally Castle, Westmeath

The *Morrigan*—She is also known as Morrígu, is a classic triple goddess, with varying names. The most common set is Badb, Macha and Nemain, together known as the Morrigna. She is known by many other names and appears in many of the Tuatha dé Danann tales as a crow, a cow, or a wolf.

It is thought the Morrigan's breasts fed the other gods, and she is one of the wives of the Great Dagda. She is associated with prosperity, strife, sovereignty, death, war and motherhood. During a battle of the Tuatha dé Danann against the Fomóire, she breaks the fighting with a battlefield poem, and then chants another poem celebrating the victory and prophesying the end of the world. Her role often has premonitions of a warrior's death, and she is perhaps associated with the banshee for this reason. She is not a goddess to be scorned or rejected, as Cú Chulainn discovers, nor is she kind or sweet.

Brigid—also seen as Brid, Brigit, or Brighid, she has morphed from Goddess to Christian Saint quite seamlessly. She is associated with February 1, St. Brigid's Day or Candlemas, and represents the light showing spring the way back from winter. This day is also known as the pagan holiday of Imbolc. She is the daughter of the Dagda and has two sisters of the same name, another triple goddess. She is a healer, a smith, and a poet. She is associated with flames (both candle and the blacksmith's hearth). She is a protector of childbirth and rules over high places. There was a 1,000-year-old (at least) shrine to her which held an ever-burning fire, guarded by first priestesses and then nuns, in Kildare. It was extinguished a couple of times throughout history, by Henry VIII, and by Henry of London, Archbishop of London, but was relit by others, and the tradition continues to this day.

Brigid has many holy wells dedicated to her, one of the largest at Kildare, which has a statue of her holding a sacred flame, and a wishing tree, or clootie tree. Tradition asks you to tie a piece of ribbon or cloth on the tree, then make a wish, as this bit disintegrates from the tree, your wish is released to the goddess.

A Brigid's Cross is made of rushes or straw in a square-shaped cross and is hung in the home for protection from evil spirits. This is now a Christian symbol, but probably came from a pagan sunwheel, and was kept because of the cross shape.

There are many crosses in pre-Christian European lands, by the way. The great stone circle at Calanais, on the Isle of Lewis, Scotland, is in the form of a great even-armed cross. This was a sun symbol to the ancients and held sacred to many people.

Cailleach—(kay-lek) is considered a crone goddess, embodying wisdom, magic, and cruelty. She is portrayed as an old woman, the Veiled One, or the Death Hag. She is a guardian of the underworld, holding winter as her season and earth as her element. She may represent deified ancestors.

Birr Castle, Offaly

She is also present in Scottish and Manx mythology and predates the arrival of the Celtic gods. She pairs with Brigid, ruling the cold half of the year while Brigid rules the warm half. If the weather is nice on Brigid's Day, it means the Cailleach is able to go out and gather more firewood, and winter will last longer. If the weather is foul, then the Cailleach is asleep, and winter is almost over. After the grain harvest in the fall, a farmer should make a corn dolly, which represents the Cailleach, from the last sheaf of the crop. This dolly is cared for each year; feeding the hag' all winter, and then burned in the Bealtaine fires.

On the Cliffs of Moher, there is an outcropping called Hag's Head, named for the Cailleach, and there is a passage tomb called *Sliabh na Caillí.* It is possible *Síle na gcíoch* (Sheela-na-gigs), figurative carvings of women displaying exaggerated vulva, are derived somehow from the legends of the Cailleach. The Ring of Beara may also be named after her, as the *Cailleach Bheara*.

Lugh—(pronounced lew) Was the Shining One, the sun god. He is also portrayed as having good humor, and perhaps even a trickster. Thunderstorms are thought to be the battle between Lugh and Balor.

It was prophesied Balor's grandson would kill him, so Balor, a Fomór, kept his daughter, Ethniu in a tower. Of course, this never works in legends, and she is found by a man of the Tuatha dé Danann, falls in love, and conceives. When she gives birth, Balor takes the triplets to have them drowned, but one falls out of the bag (Lugh) and is fostered by a smith, a bard, and many others, and becomes a master of all crafts. He then has to prove himself at the Tuatha court, and becomes the advisor to High King Nuada, Chief Ollamh of Ireland. He helps them rise and defeat their Fomóire overlords.

Lugh had a spear which is magical, as well as a sling stone which kills Balor, his grandfather, thus fulfilling the prophecy.

He also has a horse who could ride over land and sea, furnished to him by *Manannán mac Lir*, God of the sea, and a coracle (small boat) called Wave-Sweeper, which would carry as many people as it needed to.

Cavan

Lughnasadh, (LOO-na-sa) the pagan festival held around the first harvest, or August 1, is named for him. He started the festival in honor of his foster-mother, Tailtiu. *Lúnasa* is now the Irish name for the month of August.

SAINTS

While the Irish, being a strongly Catholic nation, honor many saints, there are three which stand out as being patron saints of Ireland. The obvious one is St. Patrick, but others are St. Brigid and St. Columba.

Saint Patrick

Patrick was not, according to Roman records, Irish. He was the son of a Roman deacon and grandson of a priest, living in what is believed to be modern-day Wales. He was captured at age sixteen and taken as a slave to Ireland to work as a shepherd. He was evidently not very religious before this, perhaps even a bit of a delinquent, but found solace in faith during his lonely days and nights on the hills. When he did escape, after six years, it was thanks to a vision he had. He found a ship and returned home.

The escapee followed his new religious path to study in Rome. Patrick then had a vision that he should go back to Ireland and help them become Christian. He concentrated on converting the kings, believing (rightly) that eventually the peasantry would follow.

He was moderately successful, but as Ireland was a seething mass of independent kingdoms at the time, it likely took a great deal of time and effort, traipsing across a forest-covered land of tiny, warring kingships. He was based in Armagh, in today's Northern Ireland.

We've all heard the legends where St. Patrick banishes the snakes from Ireland. According to biological archeology, there have never been snakes on the island. However, this is commonly understood to be an allegory for the conversion process, as the pagan religion and Druidry are often associated with the snakelike Celtic knotwork.

Another legend about Saint Patrick regards using the shamrock to demonstrate how the trinity is really one entity, and thus giving rise to the shamrock as being a symbol of Christian Ireland (the national symbol is the harp). There is nothing in his writing of this practice, but the shamrock had been sacred in pagan times, as a representation of the triple goddess, which I find rather ironic.

Patrick was not, as commonly believed, the first Christian missionary to pagan Ireland. Palladius had been sent there beforehand to administer to already-existing Christian communities, and Saint Ciaran lived there in the latter half of the fourth century. However, they laid a basic groundwork Patrick could then use for his own conversions later.

Saint Brigid

As we saw earlier, Brigid is originally a goddess in Irish pagan belief, and she is successfully morphed into a saint by the Christianized Irish. There is probably at least one, if not eleven, historical figures who lend their history to this saint's story. She was known to be an early Irish Christian nun and abbess in the late 5th and early 6th centuries. She established many monastic settlements, but she is most widely associated with her settlement in what is today's town of Kildare in the heart of County Kildare. Her feast day is February 1, which is also the pagan celebration of Imbolc. On this day, town locals hold memorial events, and special masses are said in the church which bears her name.

Larne, Antrim

Some sources list her as having been from Dundalk, and her father, *Dubhthach*, a king of Leinster, was a pagan. Her mother was a Christian Pict named *Brocca*, who had been a slave baptized by Saint Patrick. Other legends say Brigid is the daughter of a Druid, and threw up any sustenance he fed her, so she had to be nourished directly from a cow. She is accredited to many miracles, including the healing of leprosy, curing two dumb sisters, and magically restoring a stock of butter she had given to the poor from her mother's supply. She also is said to have cursed a nun who withheld her charity from lepers.

Rare as it was in medieval society, she appears to have been a woman of some power. She became the head abbess in Ireland, in charge of many religious centers throughout the land. Brigid founded a school of art, metal work, and illumination, and perhaps helped create the Book of Kildare, an illuminated manuscript similar to the Book of Kells.

Brigid is particularly associated with Kildare, and as mentioned in the Gods section, has a holy well there, a statue, and a wishing tree. She also has a sacred flame dedicated to her which has been maintained almost continuously for over 1,000 years. There are other holy wells throughout Ireland dedicated to her. You will often see a little sign pointing the way to one, hidden in a fold of the earth, or under a tree.

There is a well near the Hill of Tara, for instance, and another near the Cliffs of Moher. Take the time to seek out the holy wells, and perhaps make a dedication, a prayer, or a wish. Brigid is definitely a very motherly saint or goddess, whatever your beliefs, and she takes good care of her people. Perhaps if she had been a man, she would have become the patron saint of Ireland in Patrick's stead.

St. Colmcille's Well, Offaly

Saint Columba

In Irish, his name is *Colum Chille*, or Dove of the Church. He was an Irish missionary who is credited with bringing Christianity from Ireland to the Picts in Scotland during the 6th century. He was also a king's son and a great-great-grandson of Niall of the Nine Hostages, an Irish High King of the Uí Néill clan.

As the younger son of a noble, Columba was educated in the monastery; he became a monk and then a priest. He is said to have founded several monasteries, including ones at Kells, Derry, and Swords. He argued over a psalter he had copied, and this dispute ended in a battle in which many men were killed.

Because of this, he was threatened with ex-communication, but is instead exiled from Ireland. He travels to the Isle of Iona in Scotland, where he found another monastery with twelve companions. This place remains a holy site to this day. He became a diplomat and his monastery grew to a center of literacy. From this fame, he visited with the Pictish King, *Bridei*, though he did not convert him.

Columba is recorded as having been one of the first to see the Loch Ness Monster, according to his biographer, *Adomnán*.

He performed several miracles, including healing disease, expelling malignant spirits, and calming storms. He eventually returned to Ireland later in life, where he found yet another monastery, at Durrow.

Columba was from County Donegal, and there remains today a village called Glencolmcille (*Gleann Cholm Cille*) dedicated to him. Glencolmcille is a wonderful place to visit. In addition to the religious community which still exists, there is a lovely historical village created by a local priest to help the local economy. Several cottages are set up as they would have been in the 1700s, 1800s and 1900s, offering glimpses of village life from these times, complete with hearth tools, bedding, and dishes.

Other Saints

Of course, there are other saints in Ireland throughout its history. There are far too many to list them all here. However, some others of note, or those I have come across in my travels, include the following:

Glenadalough, Wicklow

- St. Gobnait—From County Cork, she is associated with Inis Mór, the largest of the Aran Islands.

- St. Brendan the Navigator—From Tralee in County Kerry, Brendan supposedly sailed to the Americas 5th or 6th century. Noted explorer, Tim Severin, reads Navigatio Sancti Brendani Abbatis and decides to construct a boat to Brendan's specifications. He uses Brendan's notes and navigational charts and makes the same journey in 1976. Severin's Brendan Boat can still be seen today at the Craggaunowen Experience in County Clare.
- St. Fiachra—Fiachra lived in the 7th century and is today associated with gardens. There is a wild garden dedicated to him at the National Stud in Kildare.
- St. Oliver Plunkett—Oliver was a 17th century Roman Catholic Archbishop of Armagh and Primate of All Ireland who was the last victim of the Popish Plot, and the last Catholic martyr to die at Tyburn. His head is now on display in a glass case in St. Peter's Church in Drogheda, County Louth. The rest of his body was taken to Downside Abbey in England where it remains today.

- St. Kevin—Kevin was the son of a nobleman who left his life of privilege to take up Christianity. He lived as a hermit in the Wicklow Mountains where he eventually established Ireland's largest and most prolific religious center at Glendalough in the Wicklow Mountains.

Summary

As you can tell, the lines between Gods and Saints are thin and tenuous in several places throughout Irish mythology. Celtic Christianity has many pagan aspects, and the pagan tales have been heavily Christianized. I had a wonderful conversation at Brigid's Well in Kildare with a Franciscan monk in 2006. He was there to collect holy water from the well. As we talked about the various pagan aspects of Celtic Christianity, he said they are so entwined it would be impossible to separate them, and no Irishman really wished to. It is part of their cultural identity and faith.

Celtic Christianity is very different from Roman Catholic Christianity, and the Irish prefer it this way, it seems. There is, with some exceptions, a gentler feeling to Catholicism in Ireland, perhaps because the conversion from paganism was not done with flame and oppression, but with persuasion and education.

Ireland was also a haven of education and literacy through the so-called European Dark Ages, after the fall of Rome and the rampages of the barbarian tribes across the land. These tribes didn't reach Ireland, and the sacred texts, writings, and scrolls were left untouched until the Viking raiders came a few hundred years later. This is why the second half of the first millennium CE (around 500-900 CE) was called the Age of Saints and Scholars in Ireland. While there was plenty of inter-tribal war and struggle, for the most part, Ireland was left alone to prosper, grow, and most of all... learn.

Fermanagh

The Personal Facet—Friendly Folk

Powerscourt Gardens, Wicklow

The people of Ireland are the jewel in the crown of the Emerald Isle. Their hospitality is legendary, and they're deeply rooted in their history and traditions. Their odd mix of dour and cheerful could baffle the most intrigued psychologist, and yet, you cannot help but feel energized and optimistic after having a pint with one. The Irish do love their misery, and history has dealt them with many loads of it, yet they still come out fighting, drinking, and singing at the end of the day. What is the secret behind this eternal buoyancy?

I think the Irish are, in general (your mileage may vary), a practical people, but with one foot always firmly set in their dreams. While they can work and toil all their lives to keep their traditions alive, their food on the table, their Guinness in their glass, they will sing songs of lament, joy, and love in the same breath. They will put out dishes of milk for the Fair Folk they profess would be foolish to believe in. They build roads around a hawthorn tree rather than uproot it. They leave their own crowded pubs to give a stranger a lift home on a blustery night. They take a day off of work just to show someone around their corner of the island.

I shall tell you some stories of Irish hospitality. Some are short, some are long. Some are astounding, some are just sweet. All are true.

Real Estate Angel

When my friend, Sara, and her aunt were in Galway, they got into a real estate conversation with a total stranger in a bar. By the time they had to leave, the agent had given them his email and address, as well as the name, email, and address of a friend who was an estate agent, whom they should call if they were interested in purchasing a home in Ireland.

Blustery Nights in Inis Mór

My friend, Vicki, and I were on vacation in Ireland in May 2011. I had previously done a day trip (2006) to the island Inis Mór and wanted to stay longer, so we rented the Man of Aran Cottage for two nights.

It was a gloomy, rainy morning, lowering clouds and a bit depressing. We took the ferry over and huddled with the masses of soggy tourists, trying to figure out a lift to our B&B, which was near the center of the island. We finally persuaded a shuttle bus to take us over, and we settled in nicely in our warm, dry, clean room.

The cottage is a charmingly restored thatched cottage with a peat fire. It had been used in the film Man of Aran, a 1934 film about life on the island. Our room (#5) was in the next building, recently renovated with wood floors, a decent-sized room with a window overlooking the water, and a rather tiny bathroom. By tiny, I mean by US standards; it was quite normal by European standards.

Vicki was feeling tired after our long journey, so I went out to chat with Maura, one of the owners, and explore a bit. She told me Joe Watty's, a pub I was looking forward to visiting, served food from about 6 pm to 8:30 pm, and I was starting to get stir-crazy by then, I didn't travel 3,000 miles to stay caged in the B&B. So, when the sun started burning through a bit, I donned my rain poncho and went walking to the nearby shops.

I wandered into Nan Phaddy's Café to find a warm, welcoming, toasty fireplace, hot vegetable soup on the menu, and a seat near the fire waiting for me. Jeff, the organizer of a group of forty visitors from Dublin, entered after a while, and extended an invitation to join them at Joe Watty's later, even giving me his cell number. Since I was planning on going to the pub anyhow, I told him this would be great. With Vicki feeling tired, I wanted to have someone I knew already there. While I don't mind going in blind, it's much nicer if there is at least one person you've met before.

I headed back to the B&B. There was no rain for the first couple of minutes, and then it returned with a vengeance. When I got back to the room, Vicki was happily playing on her iPad. I set my clothes and jacket on the radiator to dry. This is when the sun decided to come out and start shining through, even revealing some lovely, much-missed brilliant blue patches in the sky. I decided to take advantage of the unusual weather and set out to walk the 4.5 miles to Joe Watty's. I could have called a taxi, but I wanted to absorb this rare sunshine.

Since my sneakers were soaked, I put on my other shoes and started out. The walk was long and windy, up and down hills, in and out of sun and rain. I saw several folks driving, another walker, and a biker. Along the route I also saw two donkeys, about a dozen chickens, several horses, and a gang of young hostellers.

When I got to Joe's, I saw several tables marked 'reserved' and concluded this is where Jeff's group was planning on sitting, but no one I knew was there yet. I went up to the bar, ordered myself a pint of cider and a smoked mackerel salad. The smoky, salty flavor of the fish worked perfectly with the sweet balsamic dressing. It was delicious!

There was a match on television, and everyone was very excited about it, Leinster was playing, and they won. This was evidently a good thing, judging by the cheering and other reactions. I'm rather a dunce about sports, but the mood was infectious.

Jeff and his crowd started trickling in a bit later. They were all part of a group called 'New and Not So New in Dublin', a social group which does all sorts of meetups and gatherings. I sat with and talked with several people. Fernando, who was from Mexico and just moved to Dublin a short while earlier; Maria was originally from Belgium; Jeff, the social butterfly flitted from group to group; Louisa, who had a huge plate of stone crab claws, and was somewhat apprehensive about being able to get them open; Ken looked like a younger version of Ian McShane and was an accountant like me; Declan, had lived in Thailand for a year teaching English and was about to embark on the same job in Barcelona. Declan and I both loved trivia and history, so we chatted about gaming, films, history, and many other subjects.

After everyone finished their dinner, the pints started flowing. The singer started up, we all danced and sang to songs like The Gambler, Country Roads (really? Is West Virginia so popular in Ireland??), Piano Man, With or Without You, Daydream Believer, Fields of Athenry, Molly Malone, Stuck in the Middle with You, Galway Girl, etc. The place was now packed, with at least one hen party (bachelorette party), several groups of guys, and a couple of outright stumbling drunks.

I went outside for some cooler air, as the wind was still whipping about with bits of rain. There was a pub dog playing fetch with whoever was willing to throw the straw (we couldn't find a proper stick for him). The wind was raw and wild, so it drove me back inside for more fun.

Ballyvaughan, Clare

As it neared eleven, I decided to find a lift back to the cottage, I didn't want to get stuck walking back in that weather. I made my way through the dancing crowd to the bar and asked one of the girls to ring up a taxi for me. When I went outside, an older guy in a blue van was there, one who had refused us earlier in the day, he wanted €15 for a five-mile drive. I thought perhaps he wanted to haggle, so I offered €5. I had been told €5 was normal. He said €5 wasn't even going to pay for the petrol, 'now shut the door, the weather is coming in.' Well, I went back into the pub, and asked the girl if this was really the going rate, or was he trying to gouge me? PJ, the owner of the bar, heard me, and got very upset. He said it was a ridiculous sum, and he'd take me himself.

Now, the pub was STUFFED with people. He had a great staff, but for him to leave his own pub in the middle of a Saturday night crowd just to take a tourist home was incredible. He was livid about the taxi driver and wanted to make sure this wasn't the impression I took away about Irish hospitality. PJ, you more than made up for that man's attempt to gouge the tourist. Your kindness and help is what I will remember and pass on to everyone who will listen. Thank you!

I am very glad I didn't attempt the walk back, as it was by now pitch black, and there was NO light on the route. I would have used up what was left of my cell phone charge to try to see and not stumble on some unsuspecting donkey or tumble over a dry mortar wall.

So, this was my very long story of a blustery, cold, dark night on an Irish island, and a kind, chivalric pub owner named PJ who wiped out the rude antics of the gouging taxi driver.

The Hitchhiker

Back on my 2006 visit, my two girlfriends and I were driving around our second day in Ireland. We were exploring the Burren and we'd stopped at Kilnaboy Church. Next, we headed to Caherconnell, but not without first picking up a hitchhiker.

Yes, we know, it was dangerous. But he was a little old man about 70 years old, and there were three of us. Theresa was a police officer and she said she could handle him, so we invited him in for a ride.

His name was John Rafferty, and he was from Edinburgh. He was there, walking the lands where his father came from many years ago. He was on his way to Doolin, so we took him as far as we were going (which wasn't very far, unfortunately). It perhaps saved him a half-hour walk, but we did our good deed for the day. He was a very sweet man and entertained us with a couple short stories during our ride. We felt well paid.

Gap of Dunloe, Kerry

The Jaunting Car

When visiting the Gap of Dunloe in 2006, my two girlfriends and I drove up the narrow road and found Kate Kearney's Cottage. It was about 4 pm, so we talked to some folks about taking a jaunting cart up the gap.

We so lucked out! We got Tim O'Connell and his horse Harry. Theresa and I took the cart, but the carts made Kim nervous, so she opted to ride another of Tim's horses, Susie. What a trip! Tim was chatty and incredibly nice. He lived in the gap, as did most of his family, and he'd been doing this most of his life. He owned five horses, and his father and grandfather had been doing this as well. We passed his grandmother's cottage, which was called 'Colleen Bawn'. In Irish (*cailín bán*) it means White Girl, which is an old term for a witch or a healer. Since tourists usually travel to Ireland in the winter, he usually works in Amsterdam during this time.

Kim had fun staying on the English saddle (no pommel to hold on to), and she had several conversations with Susie about where she wanted to go. Eventually she won the conversations, but it was iffy for a while, especially as Susie passed her home. It was a fabulous trip, and the visions and company were both incredible.

When we got back, we remembered we had two apples in the car, so we went to fetch those for our hard-working horses. Then we went into Kate Kearney's for some touristy shopping, music, pints, and dinner. Our earlier jaunting cart experience at Muckross House was much less enjoyable. The scenery and the trip itself were fine, but the host droned on a memorized spiel, and was much less interesting and personable than Tim. We looked Tim up again when I visited in 2011, but he happened to have the day off, so we walked the Gap instead.

The Dark Hedges, Antrim

The Photo Card

In 2006, I was in Killarney, and my travel companion, Theresa, needed to transfer the photos from her data card to a

CD. We found a shop for this right across from Danny Mann's Pub. The guy was very helpful and made sure they were done right. We went to check our email at a nearby internet café while we waited. Going back to the photo place, the guy (Tom) couldn't get the larger card to read, so he asked if he could do so overnight off-site. We said we'd be back tomorrow to pick it up. Since Theresa was still interested in 'afternoon tea', we asked if there was any place nearby. He suggested 'Jams' around the corner, but it looked more like a café than a place for a formal afternoon tea.

Theresa's card wasn't completed yet the next morning at the photo store in Killarney, so he told her he'd leave it at the pub across the street if we got there after he closed. Such trust! She hadn't even paid him yet!

After a day of sightseeing around the Ring of Kerry, we stopped in at the pub Tom had indicated. He was waiting at the pub to give Theresa her CD. He wanted to make sure she got it alright, which was very kind. He said he didn't feel right leaving it since it also included her memory card.

The Case of the Missing Mattress

In 2002, I visited Ireland with my husband and my parents. We had a weeklong stay at Knocktopher Abbey, a renovated 14th century abbey about twenty minutes south of Kilkenny. After a very long day of travel across the Atlantic, through London, into Dublin, and a three-hour drive, we finally made it to Knocktopher Abbey around 10:30 am, utterly exhausted and ready for bed.

We went to our cabin, which was one of a row of six attached to the main manor house of the converted Abbey. Ours was #12, the second one down, and it had two bathrooms and two bedrooms upstairs, a living room/dining room, and a kitchen downstairs. The steps were very shallow and difficult to get up and down, especially as mom has bad knees. However, after a little settling in, all of us slept soundly and long into the morning.

Dad had planned on sleeping on the pull-out couch downstairs, but discovered the mattress was inexplicably missing. I believe mom offered to sleep on the couch itself, while dad had the upstairs bedroom to himself. They both sleep with CPAP machines and are used to separate beds.

Brigit's Garden, Galway

I think we were all finally up around 10 am the next morning, refreshed, showered, and dressed. We decided today would be a relax-and-recover day and went into the office to speak with Derrick. Derrick was flabbergasted that someone would steal the pull-out couch mattress and offered to find another for us. In the meantime, though, he mentioned he had an upstairs suite in the main house that was empty all week. Would we like to use this room? Jason and I jumped at the chance, and the matter was closed.

We moved our stuff up to the third floor (second floor in Ireland) suite, which was a large efficiency-style room with two beds, a living area, a small kitchenette, and a bathroom. This way mom and dad each had their own room, and we had our own suite. Everyone was happy! Especially me, as Derrick allowed us to use the extra room at absolutely no extra charge. What service!

Nancy's Bar

Ardara in County Donegal was my favorite town on this trip. There isn't one reason which sticks out as to why it's my favorite; it just seems to be a conglomeration of all the little reasons. It's not a large place, just one main street through town with perhaps a dozen pubs and restaurants. It's near the sea, and has some fantastic sights nearby, with mountains in the distance. The people were all incredibly friendly, and I could easily move there someday. I felt at home. More than that, I felt part of the family.

Since the wind was howling and the sky was weeping most of the day (especially the latter half) we were well-wearied and weathered so decided to find some warming beverages and filling food. Our hostess at the Bay View Guest House, Marian, recommended Nancy's Bar, and mentioned there was an event going on this night. When we arrived, it was certainly crowded. When enquiring about food, we were told they weren't serving that night because of the event, but we could try the Heritage Bar. Heritage Bar wasn't serving, so we ended up with a lovely meal at the Nesbitt Arms.

Burt, Donegal

The next evening, we decided to try Nancy's again, and as we reached the door, a thin young man named Angus insisted we come right in. He mentioned my hair was fabulous (he was rather fabulous himself, which we didn't expect in such a small town in the wilds of west Ireland!), and introduced us to Daniel and Michael, who were sitting at the bar. He said Daniel was a fantastic cook, and therefore with my glorious hair, we would make a great couple. Certainly anyone could see the logic there! We settled down at a table, ordered pints and a Ploughman's Lunch of cheese, pickle, and bread for a late-night snack.

In the course of our dinner, we chatted with the men at the bar, who were quite nice, despite Angus' matchmaking attempts. Angus was apparently quite drunk and left shortly thereafter. He evidently was a star at the event the night before, dressing up as the Toucan from the Guinness ads. We enjoyed the food. It had some nice cheddar and brie, and Vicki and I fought over the bits of delicious, sweet pickle relish. A bit fell off the plate. Thou shalt not waste the pickle!

We all had a lovely conversation about politics, economics, music, etc. with everyone, perhaps a total of eight people including us. The place was much less crowded than the evening before. It turned out Daniel was a cook at the pub but was off for the evening. He was one of the sons of the owners, and Michael was a cousin. There were six children, I think, and most of them worked in the pub in some way or another. It had been in the family for three or four generations and was a very welcoming place.

The next day, after some explorations in the area, we went into Nancy's for an early dinner (or a late afternoon meal, whatever you like). I had the special, a plate of steamed mussels, while Vicki stuck with seafood chowder. The mussels were fresh and very tender, and the brown bread was soft and yummy. If Daniel was the cook today, he was quite good.

While we were eating and catching up on our impressions of the day, one of the sisters came in with her son, Simon. We chatted with her a bit about the family.

Nancy's was a bit fuller that night, as there was a large group of French tourists in the second room having dinner. One man talked very loudly, and I could hear him over everyone else, but of course I understood none of what he said, except it sounded like the worst over-exaggerated French accent I'd ever heard.

I met a girl named Lauren at the bar. She was trying to read her book, but I kept pestering her. She turned out to be quite nice about it all, and we talked about books, history, music, and the local people. She liked science fiction, as I did, and had read the Outlander books, Narnia, etc.

I

Navan

showed her some of the jewelry pieces I made, and brought to show off to folks, and she was duly impressed. She worked as a server at a nearby restaurant, and of course knew everyone who worked at Nancy's Pub. She called it a love/hate relationship.

We alternated rounds, and I bought a pint for Alan the bartender when he was done with his shift, so he joined us. He bought me a bottle of cider while I was in the ladies' room, so I drank three bottles in total; probably a bit too much. Good thing the B&B wasn't far away!

We all chatted about the Queen's visit to Ireland that day, and how no one thought Northern Ireland would ever join the Republic of Ireland, at least not in their lifetimes. We talked about the fires which had been coursing through County Donegal a couple weeks before, and the life in a small town in Ireland. Alan ended up buying a pair of my earrings for his mother, who loved them; this was a sweet gesture. The place really made me feel as if I was part of the family. I can't wait to go back some day. When I left, the owner made sure my B&B was close by and I could get home alright. He offered to drive me there, but I was confident I could walk the half mile without problems, as I had talked a lot and drank very little in the last hour.

Nancy's is a place I will always feel welcomed and at home, and I look forward to my next visit, there WILL be a next visit, someday.

The Musical Facet—A Song and Dance

Rusty Mackerel, Donegal

Ah, the power of song, the joy of the dance. There is something universal about music, something which transcends language, culture, and prejudice. It is something which sings to our very souls. Perhaps, in some far, distant future, humankind will have a true universal language, and it will be musical in nature.

In the meantime, we listen to the songs of the Fae, the ballads of the bards, for our joyful journeys. And who does this better than the Irish? Yes, every culture has music in their history, but the Irish seem to embrace it more strongly than others. They are taught, at a young age, to sing, to dance, to play, with very few exceptions. While not all have the talent to pursue it as a career, most Irish people can at least tell a good tale, another ancient bardic art.

Let us explore this phrase, the bardic arts. A bard was a type of Druid. Druids were the priestly class in pagan Ireland for millennia. The bard told the tales, either in song or in story, of the history, myths, and legends of the people. These tales taught manners, customs, and sometimes harsh lessons. They taught of the consequences of rudeness, the folly and impetuousness of the young, and the wisdom of the aged. They stirred the blood with tales of heroism, of love, of death, and of war. Sometimes all in one tale!

The history of the last generation became the legends of the next, and those faded into the myths of the next. But they remain an integral part of the musical tradition of the Emerald Isle, and to fully appreciate their importance, you should familiarize yourself with some of the basics before you travel to this musical, magical land.

Types of music

There are four main types of music in Irish tradition; Early Irish, traditional or folk, classical, and popular. There are, of course, mutations, fusions, and crossovers in all these traditions, but when classifying such a rich tapestry of types, broad strokes must be used.

Early Irish

A bard was a much-respected member of the medieval Irish court, and as such, details of their lives were written in the official records. Thus, we have many accounts of musicians' travails, lives, and deaths going back over a thousand years in the historical records. Alas, their music usually did not survive the ages. However, it is thought several of them traveled to other lands, bringing the music of Ireland abroad, and perhaps sowing the musical seeds of the people in other places.

About 400 years ago, this tradition of court-sponsored bards started dying out, and the last great bard, Turlough O'Carolan, lived in the latter part of the 17th century and the beginning of the 18th. Many of his harp tunes have survived, are played by modern folk musicians to this very day and are considered a true heritage of Irish music. There were other musicians of this time, pipers, poets, and such, but O'Carolan is considered the last true harper of the realm. He was blind, and it was rumored he had spent some time in the faery realm, learning their music and sharing it with our world. Commonly heard covered by modern musicians are tunes such as 'Eleanor Plunkett', 'The Merry Maids of Connaught', '*Sí Bheag, Sí Mhór*', or 'Carolan's Ramble to Cashel.'

Traditional

Traditional music, folk music, includes many styles of song. They can be drinking songs, dancing songs, laments or ballads, and can be sung, played, or both. They can be reels, hornpipes, or jigs, and can be played with many instruments, including *uilleann* pipes, flutes, and fiddles. There is a style of poetic songs called *sean-nós*, or 'old style', which is usually used for laments and ballads. Sean-nós also includes singing but without musical accompaniment.

A *céilídh*, a name for an Irish dance party, would be held at someone's house or barn, and people would come of an evening and music, dance, and socialize. Most people would know many of the songs from childhood, and when folk had little money, entertainment was precious.

A revival in traditional music occurred after the Irish emigration to many countries, such as the USA, Canada, Australia, and New Zealand. Several bands in the 1960s brought this revival to the forefront, such as The Chieftains, The Clancy Brothers and Tommy Makem, The Wolfe Tones, The Dubliners, and The Irish Rovers, Christy Moore and Planxty, and The Bothy Band. I remember my mother had an album by The Irish Rovers: The Unicorn. And, of course, I can't remember a time when I DIDN'T know every song on that album by heart.

In the 1970s and '80s, more traditional bands came into the mainstream, fueling America's love for the folk tunes their parents and grandparents had known. Clannad, Altan, Danú, Sharon Shannon, Dervish, Van Morrison. These morphed into the 1990s and today, and fused into some new age, punk, and rock styles like Enya or The Pogues.

Even today, among the subculture concerts of Irish Festivals, Highland Games, and Renaissance Festivals, you can see many traditional musicians plying their trade across the world. Anywhere that has a strong Celtic influence can be home to the dulcet tones of Irish folk music. Modern incarnations of traditional groups, such as The High Kings or Celtic Woman, have brought a new vivacity to the traditional music, and brought new fans to the genre. While they are slick and modernized, they still pay homage to the original roots of the music, the message, and the tales the songs tell to new generations.

Classical

Ireland is not the first country which springs to mind when one thinks of classical music. You may think of Austria, perhaps, or Germany, or Italy, but Ireland? Yet, some of the great modern classical (if this is not a contradiction in terms) come from the modern bards of the Emerald Isle.

Most people have heard of George Handel, who was actually German and British, yet he chose to premier his Oratorio, Messiah, in Dublin in 1742 (the organ on which it was played resides in St. Michan's Church in Dublin). Some Irish born composers are John Stevenson, William Vincent Wallace, and Aloys Fleischmann. Catherine Hayes was a great singer, as was John McCormack. Today, Sir James Galway is a renowned concert flautist. Harpist Grainne Hambly is well known, I saw her in concert in Florida a couple years ago.

One production which has done much to advance both Irish dancing and Irish orchestral music is Bill Whelan's Riverdance. The singing in the original production was done by Irish group Anúna, Ireland's National Choir. This recent re-imagining of the traditional mixed with classical music, and the stepdance tradition of the island has taken the world by storm and made the art into something new and sexy.

Popular

The word 'popular' is such a broad category. It can include dance music, new age, rock, country, punk, and any number of

fusion styles. However, some of the best music in Ireland can fall under this very wide umbrella. The most successful Irish performers are, without a doubt, U2 and Enya. Other players include The Commitments, Van Morrison, Sinéad O'Connor, Afro-Celt Sound System, Kila, Thin Lizzy, Rory Gallagher, Chris de Burgh, The Boomtown Rats, Aslan, the Corrs, Westlife, the Cranberries, Cruachan, Dolores Keane, Mary Black, Sharon Shannon, and Líadan. There are, of course, hundreds more, these are just a few of the more mainstream, well-known bands, and some of my own favorites.

The Instruments

Did you know Ireland is the only country in the world to use a musical instrument as a national symbol? It's true. The harp is Ireland's symbol, heart, and soul. Do you need more proof the Irish hold music and song near and dear to their national identity? The oldest harp in the country is displayed in the Old Library at Trinity College, just after the Book of Kells exhibit, and well worth a visit.

The harp is associated with Ireland music, and for good reason. Their previously mentioned bardic tradition would have been mostly harp in history. However, there are many other instruments, traditional or newly adopted, which help to flesh out the national orchestra of Ireland.

Fiddle, of course, is strong in Irish musical tradition, and music from different parts of the country can be identified by how the fiddle music is played in the song. Donegal fiddling is fast and uses a lot of staccato bowing, while Galway fiddling is slower and with more ornamentation. More melody is emphasized in Clare fiddling.

Feadóg, the tin whistle or pennywhistle, is a simple woodwind, similar to the recorder. Depending on the key, it can be low and haunting or high and flighty.

Uilleann pipes (elbow pipes), are similar to the great bagpipes of Scotland but are played sitting down. They get their air from pumping a bellows bag with your arm rather than blowing into a pipe. This instrument is unique to Ireland. The notes are still played on the pipe, or chanter, and have two full octaves. A modern master of these pipes is Davy Spillane, who can make the pipes sing with sorrow and joy.

The *bodhrán* is a simple, hand-held drum which is usually played with a small *cipín*, or beater, sometimes with a brush on one end for more variety of sounds. Renaissance Festival bands have adopted this small, versatile drum with a vengeance.

Other instruments which you don't immediately associate with Irish music may be the Irish bouzouki, the accordion, or the banjo. However, these are very popular instruments in the modern Irish repertoire, especially in certain sections of the country.

The Dancing

When the music is thumping, who can help but get up and start moving to the beat? Especially after you've had a few pints of the black stuff, right? But it takes years to master true Irish dancing, and competition is worldwide. After the influence of Riverdance has brought it into the modern age, nearly every child of Irish descent wants to take classes. Who are we to deny them?

Irish set dancing was probably based on French quadrille dancing, and then later went on to influence American styles such as square dancing, tap, and clogging. Each part of the set dance has a tempo, such as reels, slides, hornpipes, polkas, and jigs. Some dances are 'called' in a style similar to American square dancing.

Step-dancing, however, is more solitary in performance, and also has very strict rules and forms. The upper body and arms are to remain straight; they dance in a limited space and use the staccato of their steps as part of the rhythm and music of the dance. They can be hard shoe or soft shoe, and each one has its own styles and steps. There are national and international competitions for these dances, and most dancers start at a very young age. While performers originally wore sedate outfits, today they wear outrageously bright costumes with stylized Celtic knotwork, and the girls' long, curly wigs.

However, you need to know none of this to enjoy the music and dance a reel! You can get up and dance when you feel the need. Likely there will be others doing the same.

The Songs

Now you know the background of the music, you will want to sing along when you get to Ireland, right? Definitely right. Don't feel shy. You probably already know some Irish songs and don't even realize it. Some of the songs I have heard in Irish pubs are sad, some are happy. Some are war songs, some are love songs. Any of these are available online to listen to and learn. Most are on Pandora or Accuradio Celtic stations. You can also hear some good music online from *Raidió na Gaeltachta*, the Irish language broadcast radio station in Ireland.

Sad songs: Danny Boy, Carrickfergus, Salley Gardens, Four Green Fields, The Parting Glass, Fields of Athenry, Fairytale of New York, Clare Island, the Red and Green of Mayo.

Happy songs (or at least enthusiastic): Rocky Road to Dublin, Courtin' In the Kitchen, I'll Tell Me Ma, The Little Beggarman, Whiskey in the Jar, Galway Girl.

War songs: The Green Fields of France, Arthur McBride, Danny Boy, Wind that Shakes the Barley, A Nation Once Again, Waltzing Matilda, The Foggy Dew.

Love songs: Black Velvet Band, Raggle Taggle Gypsy, Black is the Colour, Star of the County Down, Galway Girl, Spanish Lady, Red is the Rose, Carrickfergus.

Traditional pub tunes: (songs you will hear in just about any pub) Wild Rover, Fields of Athenry, Molly Malone, Spancil Hill, All For Me Grog, Johnny Jump Up, Black Velvet Band, Finnegan's Wake.

Some are simply tunes, rather than songs, Drowsy Maggy, The Butterfly, Morrison's Jig, Banish Misfortune, Toss the Feathers, and Mairi's Wedding. These are staples of most session players and are well-recognized.

Oddly enough, I have found many of my pub nights had a lot of American songs sprinkled in as well, such as Daydream Believer, Country Roads (West Virginia), and Piano Man.

Finding the Music

It would be difficult, indeed, to travel through Ireland for any length of time without coming across some of its unique music. However, it is becoming easier to come across 'prepared' performances, specifically made to entertain the tourists, glossy and polished without the authenticity of the real folk of the land. My advice is to go off the beaten path. Get out of Temple Bar and Killarney and go to a local pub which might have a traditional *seisiún*.

A seisiún (session) is a group of local musicians who have gotten together in a pub and just started playing some of the songs they all know. They may have never played together before or may do so every night. They may not even know each other, but they all know the tunes. And they are playing for the joy of playing and entertaining. They aren't being paid by the Irish Tourist Board to provide atmosphere to the Euro-laden tourist… they're having fun. No, the music may not be as high in production value, but it's more honest, and in my opinion, much more enjoyable than the staged stuff.

If you are in a city, like Dublin, where tourism is common, it may be more difficult to find the local traditional pub. Your host at the hotel or B&B may give you the standard tourist answer and direct you to a staged performance. However, if you tell them you really are interested in a traditional session, they will likely give you a better recommendation. In some places, you can just walk down the street and follow your ears. Dingle, Doolin, Ardara, Donegal, Kilkenny. I've done this in all these places. You can usually find online listings of what's going on in any given city on websites such as TradConnect.com or TheSession.org.

Music usually doesn't start until 9 or 10 pm each night. However, space is often at a premium. What I've done in the past is find a place which also serves food, eat dinner at the pub, and stay for the music. This doesn't always work well, but it's a good strategy. And of course, by the time the music starts, I have a few pints in me and enjoy the show so much more!

We usually find B&Bs which are within staggering distance of a good music pub, if we can, so we don't have to worry about the drive back to our beds. In many towns and villages, this is not a problem. If you have the scenic B&B out on the peat bog, however, you might have a problem. Make sure you have a designated driver or can ask the publican to call you a taxi to your place.

Music, to the Irish, is their very life's blood. I have yet to find an Irishman who doesn't like some sort of music and feel great pride in their bardic past. It is part of the landscape, history and soul of this delightful place.

Literature, Movies, and Shows

Tangentially related to music, or at least in the entertainment genre, are books, movies and television shows. Many have made their home in Ireland. Not only those based on the rich history of the land, but those with some fantasy or literary license. I've given a few of them below. While the scope of this book is not large enough to make an exhaustive list, I've added some of my favorites. If something is both a book and a show or movie, I've only listed it once.

BOOKS

- 1916 by Morgan Llewllyn (and many more)
- An Irish Country Doctor by Patrick Taylor
- Angela's Ashes by Frank McCourt (and many more)
- Brooklyn by Colm Tóibín
- Circle of Friends by Maeve Binchy (and many more)
- Dubliners by James Joyce (along with many more)
- Ireland: A Novel by Frank Delaney (and many more)
- P.S. I Love You by Cecilia Ahern
- Most of my books are also set in Ireland!
- The Blackwater Lightship by Colm Tóibín

- The Princes of Ireland by Edward Rutherford

MOVIES SET IN IRELAND

- The Boys from County Clare
- Bloody Sunday
- Belfast
- Black 47
- The Crying Game
- The Commitments
- Darby O'Gill and the Little People
- Dancing at Lughnasa
- Far and Away
- The Field
- Finian's Rainbow
- High Spirits
- Into the west
- In the Name of the Father
- The Last Unicorn
- Leap Year
- The Magdalene Sisters
- Man of Aran
- Matchmaker
- Michael Collins
- My Left Foot
- Omagh
- Ondine
- Patriot Games
- Philomena
- The Quiet Man
- Ryan's Daughter
- The Secret of Kells
- The Secret of Roan Inish
- Tara Road
- Veronica Guerin
- Waking Ned Devine

- The Wind That Shakes The Barley

MOVIES FILMED IN IRELAND

- Braveheart
- The Count of Monte Cristo
- Harry Potter and the Half-Blood Prince
- Moby Dick
- Once
- The Princess Bride
- Saving Private Ryan
- Star Wars: The Force Awakens/The Last Jedi

SHOWS SET IN IRELAND

- Ballykissangel
- Derry Girls
- The Fall
- Father Ted
- Moone Boy
- Mrs. Brown's Boys

SHOWS FILMED IN IRELAND

- Game of Thrones
- Line of Duty
- The Tudors
- Vikings

The Stunning Facet—
Photo opportunities

How better to capture the moment, the memory, the mood, than to take a photograph of the stunning vista you see before you on your trip to Ireland? One of the eternal draws of this island to millions of tourists is the beautiful sights which are everywhere, and it takes very little time (if any) to travel from one stunning landscape to the next. It's all contained in a compact, green package, ready to share with your envious loved ones.

Photographs provide a great service to both the photographer and his friends and family. They record the memory to share and to relive later. There are many times I've looked back on my photos and remembered a scene I had forgotten, or relived a memory I had lost. This is also a reason I write my trip reports in such detail, I know my own memory is rather faulty, so I jot down notes every time I sit down to eat during the trip. This helps me write down the narrative later and keeps my memory strong years afterwards. It also helps me realize where I took some of the photographs.

The Preparation

While there may be a few out there still using film, most people take digital photographs now, and most of those use their phone rather than a camera. If you are still on film, then some of this advice must be adjusted for this fact, so keep this in mind. However, one of the biggest advantages of digital photography is the ability to take as many photographs as you have memory space for, and sort later the ones you wish to spend money on printing. A decent digital camera before you leave deserves a bit of research. I'm not much of a movie-taker, but some people prefer video to photographs. If so, much of this will also apply to the video recorder shopping.

Giant's Causeway

The Equipment

Not everyone needs or wants a professional grade camera. These can cost over $5,000, and most people don't have this in the budget. Even high-grade amateur cameras, which usually run between $400 and $1,000, are outside most people's budget and desire. However, a decent amateur camera can be gotten for about $150-$200, and, in my opinion, are well worth the investment. You should, however, do your research, and decide which camera is right for you. If you are not planning on printing your photographs in huge sizes for hanging on the wall, your smartphone camera should be sufficient.

There is an excellent site at Digital Photography Review which allows you to choose cameras by feature and compare them side by side. I have used it many times to choose my next piece of equipment.

You will need to decide which features are important to you. Since I take a lot of landscape shots, and often from the window of a moving car, long optical zoom and fast shutter speed are very important to me. The ability to shoot in RAW format (which doesn't let the camera do any editing of the image) is also important to me, as I do a lot of post-production manipulation in Photoshop.

Is low light photography important to you, for night shots or party shots? How about close ups of flowers and other macro photography? Once you know what is important, you are ready to choose a decent camera.

By the way, some of the best shots I've taken have been from a point-and-shoot $80 camera. Good equipment is helpful but is NOT essential. The art is truly in the eye of the artist, not the equipment they use.

Brandon, Kerry

The Accessories

Many cameras come with interchangeable lenses, one for macro, one for zoom, etc. The higher-end professional cameras have this as a matter of course. The point-and-shoots do not, for the most part. The rest of us are in the middle.

My camera of choice right now is the Nikon CoolPix P900, which does NOT have a removable lens. The installed lens can zoom 83X and can do a decent macro shot. I'm happy with this range and would rather not mess with multiple lenses. This is my personal choice, and it may not be yours, so experiment with a few. Go to the store, pick up the camera with all its accessories. Do you want to be hiking up a mountain and through an airport, carrying all this? Or is it worth it to you?

Memory, memory, memory. Without it, you are done with your digital diary. Uploading to the cloud might not always be practical. There are several options to ensure you have enough on your trip. Memory sticks of any type are pretty cheap.

My option this last trip was simply to take enough sticks to make sure I never ran out of room. I never came close, even after 9,900 photos. I always, always, however, take at least one more than I think I will need, in case one gets corrupted or lost. Another option I've done in the past is take a laptop and download the card each night. This is fine if you are already planning on taking a laptop, not so much if you'd rather not carry the extra weight. Or you can post them as you take them, but again, you need good signal for that.

It's worth a note to say if you do, for some reason, accidentally erase the photos from your card, don't despair. Also, don't touch it. Don't try to take more pictures on that card. Save it until you can get in touch with an expert; he/she should be able to get most of the data from it. My friend Carla did this on our trip to Scotland. 1,200 photos were erased in the blink of an eye. She held on to it, and when she returned, she was able to get back about 90% of those precious memories she captured with the help of a data recovery specialist.

The Method

Ireland is truly a land of wonders. It is a small island, but an island which is packed with stunning seascapes, sandy beaches, rocky forts, romantic ruins, and bucolic pastures. When I went to Ireland in June 2013, in sixteen days, I had racked up over 9,900 photos. I believe in the theory you take as many photos as you possibly can on-site, as you can always sift through them later. Different perspectives, different lighting, and different levels, a couple will turn out well. You can't as easily go back and revisit the site. Even the few times I have revisited a place I previously photographed, I've discovered the landscape has changed. There is one spot, along the Ring of Kerry, where I took a photo in 2002, again in 2006, and then again in the same spot in 2011. Each time the tide, the weather, and the number of farmhouses in the foreground were different. Each was a very different photograph from the very same spot.

Conor Pass, Dingle Peninsula

In Ireland, you are tempted to stop every five minutes on your journey to take a photo of the lamb nursing by the side of the road, the ruin on the hill, the charming, thatched cottage on the road. Go ahead and do it! Do it safely, mind, there are usually small lay-bys (pullouts) which you can turn into for a very short period (don't park there, they are for passing, not parking), or driveways you can turn into. This is a country made for photo opportunities, after all! After you've seen your hundredth sheep or so, you may be less tempted to stop at the sight of each one.

You should keep in mind some basic photography truths, but also keep in mind these are rules, and rules are sometimes meant to be broken.

Gormanston College, Meath

- The rule of thirds: composition is more interesting when objects and horizon lines are on the top or bottom third of the picture, or the left/right third.
- Lines: Roads, fences, and other lines lead the eye into a particular spot. Make sure the spot has something interesting.
- Scale: The mountain photo is great, but how big is it? Take a shot with a flower, tree, or cottage in the foreground to lend

a perspective of scale.

- Weather: The weather in Ireland is part of the landscape. Use it to your advantage! There's a storm coming in, wouldn't a dark cloud look dramatic over the castle? Move your body until you can get the shot lined up right. And then run for the car before the deluge hits!
- Perspective: More interesting points of view can change the feel of a photo. Shooting straight up on a castle wall or a tree, or down on a flower can work wonders.
- Action: A standing sheep is lovely, but getting a lamb while it nurses, or a pony while running makes the photo much more interesting.
- Lighting: Sunrise and sunset, storms and clouds, and the ever-present mists of Ireland can make some amazing atmospheric shots. One reason I like staying in one place for several days is to have several opportunities to take photos at different times of the day and night.

The Locations

While all of Ireland is picturesque and charming, and different people like different things, there are certain places, subjects and areas which stand out as being incredibly photogenic.

- Cliffs—Ireland is indeed an island, and as such has a long and varied coastline. My favorite place in the world is to be on a sea cliff, looking down at the ocean crashing upon the rocks far below me. I love the mix of sea, wind, and earth, and I feel like I'm standing on the edge of the earth. As a result, I take many of my photographs in such spots. Whether it is the 1972 feet (601 meters) high, rocky sea cliffs of Sliabh Liag in Donegal, or the fine sandy beach on Slea Head of the Dingle Peninsula, I love the places where the water meets the land.
- Water—Lakes and rivers have coastlines as well, and Ireland certainly has its share of picturesque places along its waterways. The River Shannon is the longest river in Ireland

and runs through the center of the country. Many large lakes, such as Lough Derg, are on the Shannon and have stunning scenery to capture.

- Castles—Ireland has hundreds of castles, ranging from grand palaces which will rent you a room for the night to crumbling ruins which barely hold a full wall against the tide of time. Each is unique and has a photographic charm of its own.
- Some counties are more castle-rich than others, such as counties Dublin, Cork, and Clare—but there are random ruins wherever you go. Some seemingly don't even have a name, it being lost in time. Today, they are just a nuisance to the local farmer who cannot farm this part of the land.
- Critters—Sheep, cows, goats, donkeys, chickens, and horses. There are more, but these are what I see most of in Ireland. Sheep, and some more sheep. And look, there are some sheep! And a horse. And more sheep. If you visit in April or May, you will see adorable lambs running after their mothers, looking for lunch.
- Cities—Dublin has some beautiful architecture, as does Kilkenny, Galway, Cork, and Belfast, as well as the ubiquitous pubs and statues. There are throngs of people going about their merry day to photograph, and unique sites such as the political murals in Derry or Belfast, the Spanish Arch in Galway, or the Guinness Storehouse in Dublin.
- Flowers—Ireland has many incredible gardens, ranging from the Japanese Gardens in Kildare to the formal gardens in many castles, such as Glenarm or Powerscourt. Most cottages and houses have small, well-tended flower gardens in their homes, and the Irish take pride in these miniature beauties. In April and May, the countryside is awash in yellow gorse, making the landscape look like someone spilled butter across it. Wildflowers are lovely among the green.
- Cottages—Ah, the charming, thatched cottage. They transport you back to imagined romantic past lives, filled with peat smoke and traditional music. In reality, many of these are becoming impractical, but the Irish realize their

draw, and preserve those which are left for the teeming tours of photographers.

- People—Ever friendly, the people of Ireland are usually game for posing for a photograph. Especially if they are red-haired with freckles, you won't be the first to ask them! Often, after a few pints in a pub, they'll not say no. Do be respectful, though, these folk are trying to go about their day, and some are quite busy with their lives.
- 

- Stones—Yes, stones! Ireland is a very rocky country. And while the cliffs are made of stone, so are the Neolithic burial sites, the stone circles, the ogham memorials, the Celtic crosses, and the charming stone walls which crisscross along the western coast of the island. There is great texture and pattern in stones of all types. The west coast, in particular, has many of these, but they dot the entire island.
- Churches—Ireland is still a Catholic country, but many communities now have two churches, one for the Church of Ireland (Anglican) and one for the Catholic Church. Larger communities may have temples or churches of other faiths, such as Muslim, Jewish, Methodist, etc. Many churches have

also been in ruins since medieval times. Either way, they are an important part of the cultural and physical landscape of the land.

Whatever you do, do NOT be afraid of walking off the beaten path. Climb into the forest, up a rock, into a graveyard, around a stone wall, the possibilities are endless. Of course, be aware of your surroundings and dress appropriately for your adventures. Bring what supplies are required, such as walking sticks, sturdy shoes, water and food, etc.

If you are truly adventurous, go on a mountain walk with someone like Nicky at The Antrim Rambler. Keep in mind some sites, like the Ballycrovane Stone in West Cork, or the Kilclooney Dolmen in County Donegal, are only accessible if you walk THROUGH someone's yard or field. This is allowed but do be respectful with the owners' permission (as this may be a working farm or other place of business and do no harm to the property.

The Aftermath

Inevitably, you get home and look at your photos, and you are disappointed. You remember it being much more breathtaking than the photo could capture. This is, unfortunately, due to the limitations of modern technology.

While today's cameras are incredible, they still are not the human eye, and can only capture a thin slice of the wonder we see with our own incredibly complex eye structure. Even the eye cannot truly see all our mind imagines when we look upon a fantasy landscape like Ireland. Our imagination fills the faery hills and standing stones with mystery and wonder. Our eye only sees part of this, and the camera captures even less of it.

One of the reasons I unapologetically manipulate my photographs is I want to share what my mind saw at the location, not what my eye saw, or what the camera captured. I want to share this with those who couldn't be there to experience it with me. It's a tall order and sometimes very difficult to accomplish, but I work at it until I am mostly satisfied with my results.

I usually print my photos in small format first, to see how they come out in that format (the computer screen sometimes isn't the best portrayal of what will print). I then order the prints larger to sell.

I use a company called White House Custom Copies. You can upload your photos to their server and receive them a couple days later. I've never had a problem with WHCC, and their customer service is top-notch. I've also printed canvas prints with Simply Canvas, and books and calendars at Lulu. There are many ways to share your memories with those you love!

The Tasty Facet—Irish Fare

The Irish don't have a fantastic reputation for their cooking, but this has changed in recent years. Cooking schools, such as the now famous Ballymaloe House in East Cork and Dunbrody House in County Wexford, are turning out notable chefs as Darina Allen, Rachel Allen, Clodagh McKenna, Kevin Dundon, Richard Corrigan, Kevin Thornton, and Ian Rankin.

Others are turning to Ireland's national and local ingredients, supporting local growers, and bringing back country markets. It's no wonder Ireland is fast gaining a reputation as a gourmet food nation. No more is the 'boil it all day' theory of cooking extant. Ireland is rich in tasty, juicy, incredible local ingredients; even wild foods like berries and herbs. If you think I'm the only one of this opinion, look up a show by Anthony Bourdain called The Layover and check out his Dublin episode.

Breakfasts

If you are staying at bed & breakfasts (B&Bs) and guest houses, you will likely be served a fantastic breakfast by your hosts. One option is almost always the traditional Full Irish Breakfast, aka the Full Irish, aka the All-Day Breakfast.

- This starts off with an egg (usually fried, but it can often be poached or scrambled by choice).
- Then a bit of fried or grilled bacon is added. This is not like American bacon. This is a cured pork loin, thinly sliced and fried or grilled. They call our type of bacon 'streaky bacon'.
- Add a couple of link sausages called breakfast sausages. These are usually not very spicy or peppery.
- Black pudding, a slice of blood sausage made with grains and

spices.

- White pudding, like black pudding, but with liver instead of blood.
- Hash browns or potato cakes.
- Grilled half tomato.
- Grilled mushrooms.

Items usually available on the sideboard, such as Irish soda bread, whole-grain brown bread, traditional toast, various cereals, yogurt, fresh or stewed fruits

Other options include smoked salmon with scrambled eggs, oatmeal (aka porridge), cereal, fruit, poached eggs, and often many of the sideboard items included in the Full Irish listed above. In addition, coffee, tea, milk, and often several types of juice are available. Sometimes there are homemade jams and jellies, scones, and in some of the larger guesthouses, pancakes (both Irish style and American style), French toast, and Belgian style waffles as well. And did I mention the Irish soda bread, food of the Gods.

You will NOT go away hungry from an Irish breakfast. More likely, you won't be hungry again until 2 or 3 pm, at which point, most places will no longer be serving lunch, so eat less and have a normal lunchtime, or be prepared with snacks to keep you until dinner.

Food

Modern Western civilization is very much a food-oriented culture. We ritualize the need for sustenance so much, it is difficult to find ways to socialize without food or drink as an integral aspect of the event. Parties have drinks, dates have dinner, and family gatherings are for holiday meals or barbecues. We obsess about food; the presentation, the taste, the style, etc. So, let us dedicate some space to the Irish take on the subject.

When I go to Ireland, the pub is my usual stop for food, be it lunch or dinner. Part of this is because they are more often open at the times, I am hungry, rather than just a few hours for lunch or dinner. Part of this is because I enjoy a pint with my meal. And part is just because I love going to pubs and talking with folks.

Traditionally, pubs have been primarily for drinking, with snacks as an afterthought. Pub grub, such as crisps or peanuts, was simply there to help drink sales. A Ploughman's Lunch (bits of cheese, relish or pickled vegetables, and some bread) is a holdover from this time.

This got upgraded to 'toasted specials and a pint' places in the 1950s, still not requiring a full kitchen. Then it expanded to include fish-n-chips, steak and ale pie, bangers and mash, and on the odd occasion, pasties.

Since the 1990s, however, many pubs have become Gastropubs, and delight in a full menu of gustatory delights which rival the quality and variety of 'normal' restaurants. Even so, there are certain dishes you will find at almost any pub worth its salt in Ireland.

- Irish stew—chunks of tender lamb in a cream or chicken broth, with chunks of potato, celery and carrots. I have seen it with tomato on occasion. If there is a national dish of Ireland, this is it. In touristy establishments, beef might be substituted for lamb.
- Fish-n-chips—battered and deep fried, flaky white fish and thick cut chips (fries).
- 

- Mussels—especially on the west coast, mussels in garlic sauce are a staple.
- Beef & Guinness stew or pie—a savory dark brown stew

with chunks of beef, potato, and carrot. I've also seen it with lamb.

- Deep fried mushrooms—often with Aioli sauce.
- Goat's cheese salad—sometimes the cheese is fried, sometimes baked, sometimes cold. Usually served on salad greens and a sweet chutney of some sort, like cranberry compote or peach salsa, and with a balsamic vinaigrette dressing.
- Soups—unless it is a 'stew', it will likely be pureed. Vegetable soup, potato soup, mushroom soup, etc. These are more than likely to come as a creamy puree, so be warned.
- Ploughman's lunch—bits of artisan cheeses, some breads (often Irish soda bread), butter, some relish or 'pickle' of various types, and perhaps some pickled onion or a pickled egg.
- Colcannon—mashed potato, cabbage, and butter.
- Bacon and cabbage—boiled collar bacon or bacon loin, the cabbage is then simmered in the meat liquor until tender Often potatoes will be cooked in the same liquor, as well as carrots.
- Shepherd's Pie—mashed potatoes, topped with minced meat (usually lamb, as beef is called Cottage Pie) and vegetables.
- Burgers—yes, lots of burgers. Chicken sandwiches abound, as well. Usually these are made with high-quality beef and lots of topping choices.
- Sticky toffee pudding—a light sponge cake covered in a butter rum toffee sauce, usually served hot.
- Bannoffee Pie—a banana toffee cream pie.

If you would rather not eat at the pub, the traditional-style restaurants are great, as well. I'm a big fan of seafood, and Ireland has wonderful dishes made with salmon, prawns, mackerel, mussels, and oysters. Their beef is top-notch, but I usually go for the lamb, as it is more difficult to find in the US, and it is everywhere on the menu in Ireland, especially in spring and summer months.

Their ethnic restaurants tend to be delicious as well, some of the best Indian and Chinese food I've had has been in Ireland and Scotland. However, I tend to stay away from some dishes. I've been disappointed with Irish attempts at barbecue or Cajun food, for instance.

Ironically, national polls for the nation's favorite food have resulted in Thai Green Curry many times.

Street food is also an option. I've had Irish pancakes, 99s (soft ice cream cone with a chocolate Flake; a small stick of swirled ribbons of chocolate), fish-n-chips, and doner kebabs (this has layers of meat, usually lamb, pressed onto a central pole and pressed, cooked, then shaved to put into pita bread with condiments).

Or you can get supplies at the grocery store to make food for later or have as a snack on the road. If you are staying in a self-catering place, you will likely have a kitchen and fridge available to make your own creations from groceries bought at the local farmer's market or shop.

Drinks

As the Irish have made their mark on the culinary world, they also have a reputation for drinking. Many of the jokes about the Irish involve their penchant for drinking, and then fighting, and then drinking some more.

Not drunk is he who from the floor
Can rise alone and still drink more
But drunk is They, who prostrate lies
Without the power to drink or rise
- Thomas Love Peacock

An Irishman's true love is his drink. But which one? There are many choices.

Whiskey is often a first choice. From the Irish words *Uisce Beatha* or Water of Life, whiskey was first distilled by monks over a thousand years ago and is today popular all over the world. Many of the Irish distilleries are open and available for tours, such as Old Bushmill's, Tullamore Dew, Killbeggan, and Jameson's. They can be blended or single malt, and served straight, on the rocks, or mixed with something (though most Irishmen will look at you askance for the latter request).

Guinness, or The Black Stuff, is a heavy porter or stout beer started by Sir Arthur Guinness in 1759. The brewery in Dublin has a great tourist track through to the top, where you can get a free pint at the source. It is available on tap everywhere, and you can get it in half pints if you don't feel up to the full pint. Other beers are available, of course, such as Murphy's and Beamish (both stouts brewed exclusively in Cork City), Smithwick's or Kilkenny. You can also get all sorts of imports, from Budweiser to Grolsch. And don't forget micro or artisan breweries such as Kinsale Brewery, Biddy Early, Burren Brewery, Porterhouse Brewing Company, etc.

Cider is my personal favorite, as I don't care for the bitter taste of beers and am too much of a lightweight for whiskey. Cider, aka hard cider, an apple-based alcoholic, carbonated drink, most often served in bottles in Irish pubs. The most common brand is Bulmer's, or Magner's in Northern Ireland.

Cream liquor, the most commonly known being Bailey's, is usually available at pubs. There are many brands which are, in my opinion, better than Bailey's, such as Carolan's or Columba. They are often served on ice or as a shot in coffee.

Mead's favor has waned since Viking times but is resurging in popularity. It is a very sweet honey wine, and while some are dry, most are much sweeter than the 'sweet' white wines.

Poitín is a distilled spirit made from potatoes and is basically Irish moonshine. It was made illegally for centuries up in the mountains and down secret ravines to avoid the liquor duties. The result was closest to pure spirit. Today, it is being made commercially and legally available, though remarkably lower in alcohol content. Be warned, though, it is still quite potent!

Irish coffee was, I thought, an American invention like corned beef. However, it was actually invented by an Irish chef after WWII at the first transatlantic airport in Foynes, County Limerick. The drink combines a spoon of sugar and a shot of whiskey poured into a cup with dark roast coffee poured gently into it. Then thick double cream poured over the back of a spoon onto the top of the coffee.

The Practical Facet—How do I…?

When you plan a trip somewhere, there are all sorts of facets to your planning. Each facet requires your attention, and ignoring one could be potentially upsetting, inconvenient, or worse. This section should help with the practical aspects of planning and enjoying a trip to Ireland. Here are some of the things I shall cover:

- How do I plan a trip to Ireland?
- When do I go?
- How much will it cost?
- Where will I stay?
- How will I get around?
- What shall I visit?
- What if something goes wrong?

Many dream about the magic of Ireland. However, many do not grab this dream, why not? 'It's too expensive,' you say. 'I could never afford a trip to Europe.'

Less expensive than a week at Disneyworld, I say. While prices change constantly, I can give an example of a trip we took. For two people on a two-week Ireland vacation in summer, including airfare, rental car, B&B lodging and trip insurance, we spent about $1,600 per person. Yes, that's it.

Now, this doesn't include food, petrol (gasoline) or souvenirs, of course, but it did include a wonderful vacation to a *truly* magical place. And keep in mind, if you go to Northern Ireland, it may be more expensive.

Northern Ireland is part of the United Kingdom and operates on the British Pound Sterling which has a different exchange rate than the Euro against the dollar. Also, prices change all the time, especially for airfare. In 2013, the airfare that I got for $800 in 2006 is now closer to $1,000, and that was back down to $800 in 2022, but sales happen all the time.

Since COVID-19, costs of many things have gone up, so everything is still in flux. Rental cars, in particular, have skyrocketed, due to companies selling off excess inventory during the pandemic.

So, how do you get such a deal? Well, it takes patience, research, and the ability to make decisions when you need to. I will take you through, step-by-step, how to get the best deal for an Ireland vacation.

DECISIONS: Who, What, Where, When, How, and Why.

WHO

WHO's going? You? Your spouse? Your children or parents? Your best friend? A huge group of twenty friends? (not recommended unless you want ulcers) This decision makes a big difference in lodging and transportation choices. I have learned, through trial and many errors, there are certain people who travel well together, and those who don't. For instance, I will no longer travel with a mixed group of friends, spouse and/or family. I have determined, in order to keep my sanity, I shall only travel with one type of companion at a time. Otherwise, I become a funnel through which all complaints about others are poured. Choose wisely to avoid problems.

WHAT

WHAT to do? Are you interested in touring the whiskey distilleries? Ruined abbeys? Pubs and charming villages? Your trip doesn't have to have a theme, of course, but it is more fun if you have one, and helps you to plan when your mind is blank. Perhaps you've seen a movie or read a book set in Dublin, and want to tour the area? Or you dance and want to learn step dancing or how to play the bodhran? The imagination can take flight.

Ballinskelligs Beach, Kerry

WHERE

WHERE to go, of course, depends on WHAT you are doing. It also ties into WHEN you want to go. It probably needs to be considered as a package deal, so to speak.

WHERE includes the character of place: Towns and villages, or bustling metropolis? Mountains or patchwork hills? Coastline or lakeside? While each city has its own character, they can be overwhelming at times, and aren't always the best places to stay, much less drive. A small village used as a base of exploration can be wonderful, and you get more chances to meet the locals. More details on this decision are explored under 'WHY' below.

WHEN

WHEN is an important consideration. While the weather is, on average, nicer in the summer, and the days are longer, the trip will also be more expensive and more crowded. Alternatively, the winter is cheaper, and you have things more to yourself, but the weather is harsher, most traditional tourist attractions will be closed or some natural sites inaccessible in poor weather. Also, the days will be much shorter (an average of five hours of daylight in fair weather).

It's up to you to determine your comfort zone. The peak season is June, July, and August. The shoulder seasons of April, May, September, and October may offer the best of both worlds. These months are my preferred time for traveling. Except for right around Christmas and Easter, the winter months of November through March offer the best deal, but the highest possibility of weather difficulties.

HOW

HOW are you going to get there, and HOW will you get around once you are there? Usually, the easiest answer to the former question is via airplane. Airfare will be a good chunk of your travel budget, but with some research and patience, you can find a decent fare.

Faunkill Woods, Cork

Keep in mind that some websites quote the base fare only, and then have taxes and additional fees, such as for baggage, so make sure you are comparing apples to apples when doing your research. There are several sites I go to in order to find comparable flights, such as Kayak and Googleflights. The cost is usually more expensive from smaller airports, and from farther away, such as California, as compared to east coast departures.

The latter question, of travel once you are on the ground, has more options. While my favorite, by far, is to rent your own car and wander around the green hills on your own, this is not the only option. You can travel to many of the major cities by train or go via tour bus (either an all-inclusive tour or shorter day trips).

You can even rent a traveler's-style wagon to see some of the more remote areas. You can also rent a boat to sightsee along Ireland's waterways. You can also hike or cycle. However, the vast majority of folks will want to get a car.

RENTING A CAR

This is probably the toughest, most confusing part about taking a trip to Ireland, and the rules change often. Do not be dismayed by the wealth of conflicting information out there! While the rules change, there are some basics which need to be covered.

As I mentioned earlier, COVID-19 has made rental cars scarce and expensive. I recommend researching early, reserving early, and check often to ensure you have a good deal.

Most credit cards issued in the US do NOT cover insurance on vehicles rented in Ireland. There are a few cards still left which MAY cover Ireland rentals, such as some World MasterCards, but you must check with your card, and even then, the clerk you speak to may not know the truth. Call and speak to your MasterCard representative (that's the insurance agent for MasterCard).

Have them send you a letter saying you are definitively covered in the Republic of Ireland, or the rental agent may deny you have coverage. Another thing to consider, if renting in the UK (which includes Northern Ireland), and the Collision Damage Waiver (CDW) is covered by your credit card, be aware most cards only cover value up to $50,000.

If you do not have coverage on your credit card, you might be able to buy it as part of your trip insurance. Go check out *Insure My Trip* to see your options, and some will have the option of covering your rental car. Make sure it's valid in the Republic of Ireland, though, as the rules change for Northern Ireland. Otherwise, CDW insurance must be purchased from the car rental agency. In and of itself, this is not traumatic, but it can add a large chunk of change to your total rental cost, so if you can get coverage elsewhere, it will save you money.

Also, if you get coverage from someone other than the rental company, they may put either a hold on your credit card for several thousand Euros, or actually charge a deposit to the card, to be refunded when you return the car in good order. While this sounds like the same thing, it is not, as many credit cards charge a 2-3% foreign transaction fee for any transaction. This would be charged twice for a deposit and a subsequent refund, so you would be out this fee twice. Be prepared.

You also have the option of purchasing additional insurance, sometimes called SuperCDW, from most rental agencies. Usually (not always!) this will decrease your deductible, sometimes to zero. This added insurance usually covers optional things, like side mirrors, tires (tyres) windshields (windscreens), and undercarriage, which may not normally be covered. So definitely read all the fine print.

My new favorite rental agency is Conn's Ireland Rentals. They are an Irish company with decades of experience and reputation behind them. They pride themselves on quoting you ALL costs up front, nothing hidden, no whammies when you sign. Trust me, this is a huge advantage over the other companies. They can usually pick you up from the airport and drop you back when you return the car.

Michele at Ireland Yes has a great discussion thread in her forum about these issues.

An Port, Donegal

You might also want to think about WHY you want to go. Do you want to touch the roots of your ancestors? Or experience an ancient culture? Have you always felt an unexplainable pull to Ireland? Or do you just want to get away from the screaming kids or make your co-workers jealous? There are many reasons WHY you may want to go to Ireland. Pick several!

RESEARCH: Find out everything about everything—then throw half of it away

The internet is many things. Addicting, yes; maddening, yes. But it is also incredibly helpful when doing research, especially about places far from your home. Airfare, lodging, car rental, and destinations like cities, beautiful beaches (yes, they exist in Ireland), and gloomy castles are all listed somewhere; you just have to find them. The best order of research I've found is as follows:

- Make up a crazy wish list, anything you (and your traveling companions) have any interest in seeing.

- Decide which items are your 'must sees', those places you have your heart set on.
- Plot these 'must sees' out on a map of Ireland.
- See if you can construct a basic progression itinerary from those spots, incorporating the non-'must sees' when you can.
- See if you can find airfare in and out of places logical for the itinerary.
- Research lodging along the way.
- Research ground transportation.

The airfares available may define your itinerary somewhat, and the itinerary will help define the other items.

Maghera Beach, Donegal

Itinerary:

There is a wealth of information about places: castles and manor houses, historical monuments, special interest workshops, battle sites, and other places of interest. Most cities and towns, even villages, have their own website with tourist information.

In addition, many travel agent websites have great information for the intrepid traveler. Even more, there are websites dedicated to those interested in travel, with wonderful forums for those odd questions. Some of my favorites are listed in the Maps and Resources section at the back of this book.

Once you have done exhaustive research of the places you want to see, throw half of it out. Yes, that's right. You will likely end up with a list of seventeen things to see in each location, but you will only have time for a third of them, so pick your favorites.

O'Brien's Tower

Also, do yourself a favor by leaving room in your itinerary for free time, wandering around and getting lost, people-watching at a café, or just having a pint with the locals. These are usually the most memorable parts of your trip, so leave time for them.

You don't want to end up with an itinerary where you are rushing through things so fast you don't see them. Michele at Ireland Yes calls this the Green Blur Tour. While some people prefer a fast-paced vacation, it does sometimes pay off to stop and enjoy what you are seeing, rather than just marking off things you've seen on a checklist: Blarney Castle? Check! The Cliffs of Moher? Check!

If you've got the places listed you want to see, look for a pattern. Are they all close to a couple central locations? If so, pick several places and use them as bases of exploration around that region. Or can they be strung together in a circle over a larger region? If so, spend a couple nights in each place, moving around that circular route. Plan wisely and try to avoid crisscrossing or backtracking. Check driving times between places with Via Michelin or Google Maps.

Then add about 25% to those driving times, as mapping programs don't take into account Irish roads. They twist and turn, which keeps speeds down lower than the speed limit. They have hills and valleys, sheep, tractors, and occasionally cows, or even road works.

You don't want to spend all of your time driving, trust me. It gets very tiring, especially as you will likely be driving a manual transmission, which are the majority rental cars available (automatics are available at a higher cost, often double). I try to keep my days to three hours of driving at the most, and break up the blocks of driving with sites along the way.

I find the most reliable way to figure a distance is estimate your speed at 35mph on average. Then add some time for stopping for lunch, photo opportunities, bathroom breaks, and exploring the side street where you saw a cute cottage. Was does that sign say? Let's see where it goes!

If you enlist in a travel agent to help you design an itinerary, be sure to ask about the agent's personal experience in Ireland. It's quite common for agents to sell custom itineraries even if they've never visited Ireland themselves. Therefore, they have no real experience on the roads. Be sure to work with a professional who specializes in Irish travel and has hands-on experience and knowledge as a local would.

Airfare:

This is usually the biggest chunk of your travel budget, depending on where you are traveling from. There is a definite season to visit Ireland: summer. While many people do go during the 'peak' months of July and August, there is indeed a reason why summer is the best. The days are longer to see sights, warmer weather, less rain and wind, and everything is open.

This also means the airfare is the most expensive, as well as hotels. Smaller lodging, like B&Bs and guesthouses, have much the same rates year-round.

The shoulder months of April, May, September, and October are becoming more popular, as the weather is still usually decent, and the days aren't incredibly short yet. However, this also means the airfares are creeping up as these become more popular times to travel.

I've traveled to Ireland in April, It was beautiful and inexpensive. Please note some places won't be open in the shoulder and off seasons, many B&Bs, some restaurants, and most attractions may close after October and remain closed until around March. If you are in doubt, check first to see if your 'must see' sights are open before making definitive plans.

Slane Castle, Meath

When I've decided on what I want to see and where I want to stay, I look for the nearest airport(s), then start researching my flights. I go to dozens of websites, sometimes daily to watch fares before buying. I found good fares on Travelocity on a one-day fare sale through Virgin Atlantic. When I planned my last trip, the tickets were non-stop from Miami to London for just $488 including taxes in June. They were gone within 24 hours, so if I hadn't jumped on them, I would have been stuck with the $800 per ticket. Do your research. There are deals out there.

Also consider flying into one city and out of another. This is great for Ireland, as you can fly into Shannon, explore the west, and end up flying out of Dublin at the end of your trip. Edinburgh, London, and Glasgow are also considerations for this technique. This is called an open-jaw ticket, and usually doesn't cost much more, if any, than a normal round-trip ticket.

There are others, of course, but these are the ones I've used most often. Also don't forget to check the airline websites; if you find a great fare on Expedia for Delta, Delta might have it cheaper on their own site, and it is usually better to deal directly rather than through a middleman.

Some airlines, like Aer Lingus, or Southwest (which isn't international, but could get you to a hub like New York cheaper) may not be listed on price consolidation sites like Travelocity, Kayak, or Expedia. Check those sites on your own.

I sign up for airfare alerts when I'm researching fares, so I get quick notification of sales. Airfarewatchdog is a great place to keep track of a particular fare, as the site follows fares rise and fall. You can set up email alerts for when the price rises or drops a particular amount or to a particular level. Some of the consolidation websites do this as well.

Also remember not all sites include taxes in their fare quotes. I sign up for airfare alerts when I'm researching fares, so I get quick notification of sales.

When you buy your tickets, check out the cancelation policies. Usually, the cheaper the flight, the less flexible the changes allowed. Make sure you are going before you purchase non-refundable, non-change tickets. If you do have some decent reason why you might not be able to make the flight, either pay extra for flexible tickets, or get travel insurance that covers flight cancelation. Some cover delays or cancelations due to medical reasons, for instance. Keep in mind they usually mean YOUR medical reason, not a child or a parent for whom you need to stay to take care of.

Leap Castle, Offaly

Lodging:

Bed & Breakfasts and Guesthouses

Once you have your airfare and itinerary, you know which nights you need lodging and where. Ireland is wonderfully full of adorable bed & breakfasts; I highly recommend this lodging choice.

The B&Bs in the US tend to be more upscale and expensive than those in Ireland, so don't go by their example. Most B&Bs I've ever been in have been comfortable, clean, cozy, and a delight to stay. They run around €50 per person sharing per night (pppn or pps) and include a huge breakfast.

You will pay higher for city B&Bs. Where B&Bs are generally family homes, larger guesthouses are purpose-built B&Bs and can have a slightly higher cost.

Hotels

Hotels usually charge by room rather than per person. However, they usually do not include breakfast in the deal. Hotels are usually more cookie-cutter and sterile. A Hilton is the same in San Francisco as it is in New York, London, and Japan, and they lack the authenticity of a family-run B&B.

In my opinion, they are a place to stay based on convenience rather than a place to enjoy. However, there are some family-run hotels in rural areas which may offer you the privacy you want while also adding something interesting to your overall visit to Ireland, such as the Merriman Hotel in the once-smugglers village of Kinvarra in County Galway. This hotel boasts the largest single thatch building in all of Ireland.

You can also find castle hotels around the country, such as Dromoland Castle or Ashford Castle. Prices in these types of lodgings are generally more expensive but would certainly add something special to your trip, especially if you're traveling to Ireland for a special event, like an anniversary or honeymoon.

Hostels

Then you can try the other options, such as hostels (both regular hostels and youth hostels), camping, caravanning (RV), canal boats, colleges offering dormitory rooms for the summer, etc. There are plenty of unusual places to stay. Glenstal Abbey in Co. Limerick takes guests as a spiritual stay, or the Glendalough Hermitage in Co. Wicklow. Get creative!

Self-Catering

Self-catering houses are also an option, especially if you have a large group or prefer the privacy of a 'home from home' type of lodging. The biggest downfall is many require a seven-day minimum stay, usually from Saturday to Saturday. Some are willing to offer short breaks, though, so always check.

Riverboat

As noted earlier, you can see Ireland by riverboat. These are rented on a weekly or weekend basis through companies like Emerald. These boats have sleeping and some cooking facilities on board. Some companies even rent old-fashioned barges which are fully self-contained.

Once you have decided where you want to stay, make a reservation. Make sure to check the cancelation policies. If you've paid for your lodging in advance, the time you cancel will dictate how much of your money you get back.

Email is usually an option for communication these days, and I prefer this method as it leaves a 'paper trail,' and I make sure to bring a copy with me. Not everyone in Ireland is web-savvy, even if they have a website, so be patient. Some may require a phone call, most will require a credit card to secure bookings, even if it's not charged. This protects the lodging against 'no-shows.'

Don't forget the time difference. Ireland is ahead of Eastern Standard Time by five hours, and by eight hours from

Pacific Standard Time. Noon in New York and 9am in San Francisco is 5pm in Ireland. If you're organizing your trip in the evening after work, remember the folks in Ireland could be asleep.

Also, when booking your lodging, not all places in Ireland are going to take credit cards. Those which do may not take American Express. None of them take Discover.

Those which take credit cards will take Mastercard and Visa. Some are cash only, EVEN if they take a card number for the reservation. Be prepared to pay cash on departure. If a lodging is going to take a deposit or take the full amount on booking, remember you will see a foreign transaction fee on your statement. Again, check the lodging's cancelation policy if you expect a refund on cancelation.

Another thing to keep in mind is chip and pin credit cards. Not all US cards have this security option, as it's different from swipe technology, and some Irish sources require it. Do some research to ensure you have a card that will be accepted in Ireland.

Ground Transportation:

So, you know when, where, and why you are going, how are you getting around? Well, my recommendation for Ireland is definitely for renting a car, as discussed earlier. Exceptions would be if you are under or over the age limit for rentals, or if you are staying in a major city, like Dublin or Belfast the entire time (see below). In the countryside, though, while it is possible to use buses and trains to get around, and certainly many people do, you won't find this an easy option.

Irish Rail travels between cities and major towns, but a vast part of the country has no rail travel at all. Getting to the little villages and remote attractions can be difficult to impossible and very time-consuming.

If you are taking an organized bus tour, you are obliged to stick to that itinerary, so you can't make a detour on a whim to go find a hidden castle when you see a sign. You can't stay longer at one spot unless you want to get left behind; there is no flexibility.

Athlone

If you travel by public bus, you do have some flexibility in your itinerary, but you are also reliant on the bus schedule, which is often inconsistent for arrival and departure times.

Now, I know it is scary to think about driving on the 'wrong' side of the road (it's not really that difficult). It gets worse: automatic transmission cars are more expensive to rent, and the manual transmission cars make you shift with your left hand (since the driver is on the right of the car). Confused yet?

I remember many times trying to grab the stick with my right hand, only to bang it on the door. However, it's not so bad. You get used to it very quickly. The mind has an incredible ability to 'mirror' and allow you to perform the same tasks, as if mirroring the motions to what you're used to.

It helps to have a designated navigator, as the signage in Ireland is a little different from what you may be used to. Signs tell you name of the next town…in England and Irish…as well as the route number and the distance to other towns on that route. This means you should know the major towns on the way to where you are going, or even the ones just beyond your destination.

While national signs are in both English and Irish, if you are in a region known as the *Gaeltacht* (Irish speaking region), the signs will be in both Irish and English. The latter might be printed smaller, though, so learn the local name of the places.

Most folks have map apps on their smartphones. If you don't have an app, or if you don't have a data plan that you can use abroad, a GPS can still be very helpful. Not only does it help you find places (IF you have a good address for the place, not always a given, especially in rural areas), but it can definitely help you find your way BACK to your B&B if you deliberately get lost during the day, just for the fun of it. Most car rental companies offer them now, some of them even give them for free.

Cloghane, Kerry

Big cities in Ireland don't require a car to get around. In fact, having a car is a liability in Dublin. It is difficult to get around with the heavy traffic, find parking is challenging unless you know where the few multi-story car parks are, and it can be expensive both on the street and in the multi-story.

Also, Dublin has a decent public transportation system, though, and the city is quite walkable. Smaller towns and villages are often very walkable as well, and parking for the afternoon and exploring the town on foot is usually the best option. For the bigger cities like Dublin or Belfast, turn in the car before getting there, or wait to rent it until you leave.

Gas (petrol) is very expensive in Ireland. At the time of this publication, the cost is running around $5 USD a gallon. The good news is their engines run much more efficiently, and you can usually get around 45 mpg from economy size cars (larger cars get slightly lower miles per gallon). However, filling up a tank can still cost you $100 or more, so budget accordingly.

Remember the itinerary you made with estimated driving times? Use the mileage from that and double it. Yes, double it. You will be going to places, taking day trips, going out for dinner, stopping at brown sign sites, all sorts of side trips.

I would advise against renting from a place you've never heard of. Cars can be very expensive, and it is difficult to fight a fraudulent damage claim from overseas. I recommend Conn's Ireland Rentals. They are and Irish company who have been in business for a long time, are partnered with Hertz, and they offer many options.

See more on the details of renting a car, and the problems thereof, above in the RENTING A CAR section.

OTHER CONSIDERATIONS

OK, you've done your research, gotten your tickets, your reservations for lodging, and your car rental. Ready to go? Not yet!

Trip Insurance

You break your leg the week before the trip. Ruined! All your money lost! Not so, Grasshopper, if you bought the proper trip insurance. Go to Insure My Trip and compare the benefits of different packages.

Find out if your own health insurance will cover you on foreign soil. Find out if you need medical evacuation before you travel (Ireland does not require you to get special vaccinations), trip cancelation insurance in case of medical emergency, lost luggage, the above-mentioned car insurance, etc.

Compare the benefits between what you already pay for and what you need to travel and find a travel plan which fits right for your needs. For a small investment, you get a great deal of peace of mind.

Dingle

Passports and Visas

This should be taken care of before you even get the tickets, but everyone procrastinates. My husband ended up getting his passport the morning we flew out. We were very nervous, to say the least. Normal processing times for a new passport is six weeks, but please give it plenty of leeway (especially if you've already bought non-refundable tickets). This can increase to about twelve weeks without notice.

US citizens don't need visas for short visits to Ireland (including Northern Ireland which is part of the UK), but if you are going somewhere else or staying longer, do read up on the requirements long before your flight, and make sure all paperwork is in order.

Money

Ireland is on the Euro (€) system of currency. If you plan on traveling in Northern Ireland, remember that part of the country is governed by the UK and the currency is Pound Sterling (£).

Cash

I recommend going to your bank and getting a couple hundred dollars' worth of Euro as travel money for the day you land. You can get more during your stay from the ATM, and/or use your credit card for purchases. You can also get some pre-trip Euros online through companies like AAA or Thomas Cooke or order it from your bank.

Travelers Checks and Debit Cards

NEVER travel with large amounts of cash. Travelers checks were an option for many years, but now, you'd be hard pressed to find any place that accepts or exchanges them. Just... don't.

ATMs in Ireland

You can get prepaid one-time debit cards that aren't tied to a bank account if you are worried about a thief cleaning out your savings.

Be sure your bank is part of the LINK system to access your account in Ireland. Also, you may not be given a choice between linked accounts. Your ATM card will only have access to your primary account from Ireland, which is often your checking account.

You may wish to save hassle while in Ireland by opening a dedicated travel account and getting a new ATM card for that account, and make sure any and all travel funds you wish to access are in that account.

Also, keep in mind that many smaller towns and villages might not have an ATM. You may have to travel to a larger town nearby to get cash. I've also noticed some ATMs (often the only ATM in town) are inside stores, so if the store is closed, so is access to cash. Plan accordingly!

Credit Cards

Be sure to contact your bank prior to travel to let them know to expect charges made in Ireland during your travel dates. This will, hopefully, save you the hassle of having your card put on hold, or worse, canceled, mid-trip and leaving you without your card. Sometimes their fraud department will still put a hold on, but a phone call can often clear this up.

If you don't have a credit card, or your interest rate is too high, shop around for a card with a good rate. Many (Capital One is one of the few which don't) add on an extra 2% for any foreign transaction, in addition to the 1% Visa/MC charges. You don't want to carry too much cash with you, but some B&Bs, while preferring cash even if they take credit cards, require prepayment which is only taken on credit card, especially if you're calling or emailing from outside of Ireland for the booking.

You can also set up a prepaid debit card that is based on euros or pounds sterling before the trip, and use it throughout the trip, including getting cash from the ATM. I've heard of some issues with American credit cards and PINs in the UK and Ireland, and this would avoid those problems. I had one on my last trip just in case, and while it wasn't required a lot, it did help in a couple cases where a Chip and Pin card was required.

Peat bog, Donegal

Packing

Sure, you've packed dozens of times for vacations. What's the big deal? Well, the flight carry-on restrictions, for one. Transatlantic flights (well, all flights) have lots of rules, and it behooves you to know them before you are waiting in the security line for your flight.

Carry-on: Most airlines have their carry-on rules on their websites. Some have weight as well as size restrictions, and the liquid restrictions need to be obeyed. Check before you go. Right now, any carry-on liquids must be in containers no larger than 3oz (100ml) and they must all fit comfortably in a quart-sized clear Ziploc bag. Liquids include gels and semi-solid things like jellies and sometimes cheese, so be careful. When in doubt, check it in your luggage or leave it at home.

Jackets and medical equipment (like CPAP machines) are not counted towards your carry-on limits. I've taken heavy things from my carry-on and put it in my purse, which is rarely weighed. You can also stuff the pockets of the jacket. I packed some of my heavy electronic stuff, like chargers and batteries, into my CPAP machine case.

Prescription medicines must be labeled in the traveler's name; baby formula may need to be tested at the gate. You will be asked to dispose of things like uneaten food, and open bottles and cans of water or colas. There are several examples like this, so check them out on the airline's website, or better yet, the Transport Security Administration (TSA) website.

This list will also help you to know what you can bring on board to entertain yourself or your kids, such as electronic games, music players, laptops, tablets, etc. And there are new rules for smartphones. And the site will provide you with information on things like knitting needles, crochet hooks, scissors, etc.

Doolin, Clare

Checked luggage: Many airlines charge hefty fees for overweight luggage and limit the number of pieces each person can check. Also, any locks on checked luggage can be cut off by airport security if they need to inspect the bags. TSA approved locks are available in most travel sections in department stores and travel shops. Airport security has a master key for these locks if they need to access your luggage for any reason.

I usually use cable ties to secure my luggage, however, any cable ties or non-TSA locks will not be replaced by airline security once they've inspected your luggage.

Dun Aengus, Inis Mór

Don't, don't, don't put valuables or medicines in your checked luggage! I cannot emphasize this enough, yet people do it every day. Cameras, laptops, anything fragile, anything essential, must go in your carry-on.

Of course, this makes your carry-on heavy, so some decision-making is sometimes necessary, as there are strict weight limits for carry-ons. I usually put one day's worth of clean clothes in my carry-on, in case the checked luggage is delayed or lost.

If you have something really valuable, consider leaving it at home. Do you really need the diamond stud earrings on the trip, or will the cubic zirconia work? My last trip to Ireland, I did carry-on only for a sixteen-day trip. Airlines have lost my luggage too many times in the past. My trip to Scotland in 2008 resulted in me not getting my bag for five days.

Bring a soft sided carry-on or luggage, as it will likely expand with the things you buy on your trip. Some are expandable with zippered sides. Or just bring an extra duffel bag to check on the way back.

County Laoise

Jet Lag

The bane of travelers! Many people suffer from jet lag when they travel across time zones. If you are in the eastern US, you will be five hours ahead in Scotland. If you are from the western US, that increased to eight hours. While everyone's body reacts differently, here are some tips that I've followed or heard in the past that might help.

- Hydrate—drink plenty of water during your flights. This helps keep your body functioning normally and reduces travel stress. Drinking alcohol can make the problem worse, so go easy on the cocktails, as they can dehydrate you.
- Sleep—if you can sleep on the overnight trip, do so. Even if it is only a couple of hours, this will help. I usually bring earplugs and eyeshades to block noise and light. I try not to sleep very much the night before the flight, so I sleep better

on the plane. Your mileage may vary!

- Routine—I tend to go to bed an hour earlier for each of the three days before my trip. For instance, if I normally go to bed at 10pm, I will go at 9pm three days before my flight, 8pm two days before, 7pm the night before, waking earlier each morning until the day of departure. That way, your body is a little more acclimatized to your new schedule, resulting in a smaller jolt once you arrive.
- Activity—When you do wake up, make sure to try to get some sunshine first thing! This wakes up your body and lets your circadian rhythm settle in.

The day I arrive, I usually make sure to do things all day, and try to avoid napping (occasionally I give in, but make sure it's only an hour or two!). I don't plan anything heavy, like a two-hour drive or climbing a mountain. Light activity, some sightseeing, walking around the town. Then I usually crash around 9pm, and sleep like the dead.

The next morning, I'm bright-eyed and bushy-tailed, ready to tackle the world! Getting into your normal sleep pattern right away helps. Wake at your normal time and go to bed at your normal time. Even on arrival day.

Sugar levels—Invariably, my husband has a sugar crash halfway through the second day of the trip. We keep regular mealtimes and top up with power bars to counter any problems. Your body goes through a lot of stress through travel, especially if you are older or have muscular/metabolic issues, such as diabetes or fibromyalgia. Plan accordingly and make sure you have supplies on hand to combat them.

READY TO GO? Don't forget the smile!

Don't forget to pack the most important thing for any trip: a great attitude. This small item can make the worst disaster into a hilarious story and get you through a difficult situation with authorities and can take the biggest lemon and make lemonade out of it. After all, how can it be terrible. You're in Ireland!

A trip to Ireland will be full of wonderful memories, historic experiences, and meeting wonderful folks. Whether you get addicted like I have or are happy with going once and treasuring the memory forever, you will have an exquisite time.

The Frugal Facet—Budgets, Discounts, and Deals

When you are planning a trip anywhere, one of the first things you do is look at your budget for the trip. Sometimes this can be intimidating, and you are left trying to figure out how to get the most out of your limited funds and resources. This section is designed to help you find ways to stretch those resources and get the best vacation your money can buy.

Dunluce Castle, Antrim

A lot of this will depend on when you go and how long you are going to stay. A week in January is going to be much less expensive than a week in August. Airfare will be higher during the peak season of July and August, a bit lower during the shoulder season (May, June, September, October), and lowest during the winter months (except around Christmas and Easter). While it doesn't vary as much (or as capriciously), upper end lodgings will also vary based on season. Some may even be closed during the winter months, so be warned and plan ahead.

The most important aspect of finding the best deal is RESEARCH. You must spend some time to find the deals, and know enough to realize it's a good deal, and then buy it. This applies to airfare, car rental, lodging, entrance fees, train tickets…whatever you are looking for. What is a good deal? Like anything, it depends on what you're willing to pay versus how much you really want to see Ireland. But I can give you some guidelines via my experiences.

Grianan of Aileach, Donegal

PLANNING

One of the best things to do would be to visit Michele Erdvig's website, Ireland Yes. She writes a wonderful guide to Ireland, has traveled to the island more than 50 times, and updates the book every year. When you buy the book, you also get a package of coupons you can use on your trip, such as two-for-one admissions, and the like, very useful.

Another tactic is to purchase an Irish Heritage Card which allows you to get free admission to a vast list of historic properties, from medieval forts to manor houses, and so much in between. If you plan on visiting more than five of these sites on your trip, look at their list of properties to make sure if you are planning on going to those covered.

Not all historic properties are covered, so do some research. If you are spending more than a day or two in Dublin, you may also want to look into a Dublin Pass, a similar deal for the local attractions.

Speaking of Dublin, I find a great way to get a good overview of the city, and to travel around the city, is to get tickets for the Hop-On, Hop-Off (HOHO) bus which winds through the streets, stopping at various attractions and offering commentary. A good way to find them is to look for the open-top buses. The closed ones are usually for local city travel, not tourists.

Also, I recommend the live commentary buses, as the canned ones tend to be less lively and lack humor. Each time I've gone, I manage to get a host who sings for us, not necessarily very well, but with great enthusiasm. You do not need to pre-book these tours. Just show up at one of the stops, which are signposted around the city (map available at the link above).

Your ticket is good for 24 hours, so if you get on the bus at 1pm (the last tour out is a pick-up tour at 5pm), you can get back on the bus first thing in the morning for free and continue sightseeing until 1pm… though they may allow you the rest of the day if you get a nice driver.

I prefer the Dublin City Bus Tour as their guides are usually Irish, which adds to the experience. I have enjoyed the HOHO bus in many major cities, including London, Edinburgh, Dublin, New York City, and Washington DC, and always find it to be entertaining and useful.

AIRFARE

Usually, direct flights are less expensive, but that isn't always the case. Sometimes flying into or from a major hub, such as Newark or London, can help keep the costs down.

Sometimes it's the only viable option. For instance, there are no direct flights from my closest airport to Ireland. I always have to fly to a larger airport that handles jets.

I often fly open-jaw, meaning I fly into one city, like Dublin or Belfast, and fly out of another, such as Shannon. This sometimes adds a little to the cost, but not always. I tend to fly in the shoulder season, such as April or May. My tickets are usually for a Friday departure and a Sunday return.

The cost of flights fluctuates daily, so I check it often. This way, I know when a deal happens, and I grab it. I use several tools for this. Googleflights is a great one which allows you to track the cost of specific flights. I also sign up for email alerts from the airlines I might use. If you get notification of a great sale, and you know you are going, jump on it right away. That deal may be sold out in an hour!

If you are a student or a veteran, there are websites, such as Student Universe, STA Travel, or Veterans Advantage which can help you with better airfare.

Having enough frequent flyer miles with a particular airline (many credit cards allow you to accumulate these) can also either defray or replace the costs of a flight overseas. However, keep in mind many have blackout periods, and sometimes seats are more difficult to get if you are using miles to obtain them. Some airlines allow you to apply your miles to a portion of the cost, reducing the total, no matter what the seat or flight.

TRANSPORTATION

Renting a car is, by far, my highest recommended mode of transportation when traveling in the Emerald Isle. However simple this may sound, it is fraught with peril and complexity, hidden charges and downright fraud. Please see my RENTING A CAR advice in the previous section for lots of details on how to avoid, or at least minimize, them.

Another option is train travel. In Northern Ireland, a Britrail pass may be helpful. However, Ireland's trains aren't quite as all-encompassing as those in the UK. Irish Rail travels between many Irish cities, with the network starting in and often including Dublin City.

Slane, Meath

From Dublin, you can journey to such places as Belfast in the North then connect on British Rail to other destinations in Northern Ireland, such as Derry City. Within the Republic, there are hourly departures from Heuston Station in Dublin City for Cork City. Other journeys include Limerick City, Sligo,

Westport, Galway, Killarney, Tralee, Waterford, and many stops in between.

However, once you get to those hubs, you must find another way to travel around the enchanting countryside. There are actually several options; you could rent a car, a caravan, hike, find a private tour, or a larger bus tour for the area, or even rely on Bus Eireann (Irish Bus) for journeys where the train doesn't travel. It is all up to your style of travel, your budget, desires, and sometimes your physical limitations.

Unfortunately, gasoline or petrol (gas in Ireland is natural gas), is NOT cheap. It is quite expensive, averaging around $5 USD a gallon in 2055. But never fear! Most cars you rent have much better gas mileage than the gas guzzlers in the US. Diesel fuel is even more expensive, averaging $8 USD per gallon. Budget ahead of time so you aren't surprised.

LODGING

While I'm in Ireland, I greatly prefer staying at Bed & Breakfasts as my lodging choice. However, sometimes hotels are a better choice, such as the night before flying out of the airport, or in Dublin city, where B&Bs aren't available. B&Bs average $50 per person sharing per night and include the famous traditional Full Irish Breakfast.

Specialty B&Bs (historic houses, castle B&Bs, etc.) are usually a bit more expensive. I prefer B&Bs but occasionally splurge for a charming, historically significant place, or the odd thatched cottage. Keep in mind this is pppn, and therefore, twice as much for two people in the one room.

Single rooms are slightly higher, averaging $55 per night. Some B&Bs have family rooms at a discounted rate per person, perhaps $45 pppn. Again, it depends on your personal level of comfort and sharing with your traveling companions.

AirBnB is, of course, increasing in popularity all over the world. The upside is you usually pay less than in a traditional B&B. The downside is that they won't necessarily be rated by the strict B&B inspection agency.

Hotels are sometimes more economical, as they charge per room, but usually don't include the Full Irish Breakfast B&Bs in their price. However, most hotels have a restaurant where breakfast is offered, including a light or continental breakfast (toast, coffee/tea, yogurt, or fruit), a full breakfast, or a made-to-order breakfast.

Muckross House, Killarney

If you really want to splurge, you can always spend some time in a castle. Yes, you can find smaller castle accommodations than the five-star hotels. They are few but include some B&B lodging and self-catering, and sometimes a hostel.

What's the cheapest lodging while traveling in Ireland? Camping out, of course! It's not my cup of tea, but plenty of people do it, especially if they've a bike or are out hiking around the countryside.

You could also stay at hostels for a great discounted stay. Youth hostels are no longer separate from other hostels, today's difference being average hostels and specialty hostels.

Typically, hostels are purpose-built lodging with shared dorms with shared bathrooms. Hostel World is a popular site for booking around Ireland. For specialty hostel lodging, try Unique Irish Hostels.

Another option, particularly good if you've a large group, is a self-catering house. These are usually stand-alone houses or cottages, with a varying amount of space, for rent in usually week-long periods, most often from Saturday to Saturday.

Sometimes, usually off high season, you can get 'short breaks' of two to three days instead. We rented a cottage on the side of a mountain in north Cork one time, and it was a lovely place. It had been a 19th century farmhouse, refitted for rental. The outside was stone, the inside all wooden floors with an open staircase, a wood stove, and a cozy fireplace.

The tiny, winding, one-lane sheep track up the mountain to it was… charming. As were the cows we always got stuck behind on the way back to town. But these are part of the attractions to rural Ireland, and I treasure the experience.

There are several places to find self-catering lodges, but I recommend going through a well-known agent, such as Rent a Cottage, VRBO, or Imagine Ireland.

Derryclare Lough

FOOD

Food can be an expensive part of your trip, or a very cheap one, depending on your planning and habits. Staying at a B&B

can be a big part of this, the enormous breakfast your hosts will provide you should keep you fueled into the afternoon or early evening, if you let it.

We often do this, and then grab a meal late in the day for about €10 per person. Then we may have a light supper at another pub or have takeaway. Sometimes, if we are out hiking or exploring, we just grab snack foods at the local grocery store to bring with us instead of stopping for lunch. Irish bread, cheese and smoked salmon are delicious local options and are great in sandwiches made on the go.

Of course, then we get hungry mid-afternoon, only to find that many full-service restaurants are closed at that time. They typically close after 3pm and don't reopen until 4 or 5pm for dinner, so plan accordingly. Some pubs will still serve food during that time, and Takeaways are often open as well.

Late night dining (after 8pm) has a similar problem, with the same solutions. I remember one night, directly after our arrival in Ireland. We napped for a couple hours and woke at 8pm, starving. We had to go to 3 different villages before we found a place that was open and serving food that late.

If you are staying at a self-catering house, you will have a kitchen where you can prepare meals at home rather than paying for expensive meals at restaurants. Granted, you are then not offered your Full Irish Breakfast from the B&B, but sometimes all you want is a bowl of cereal or some toast when you wake up.

Some privately owned self-catering house owners will supply, at no extra cost, fresh eggs for your fridge (especially if they have their own chickens), or even the makings for a Full Irish Breakfast for the length of your stay.

DRINK

Pints are larger in Ireland than in the UK, so drink carefully. And a half-pint of beer or cider is about the same price as the same amount of soda, so enjoy your drink! Don't dare drink and drive, though. The penalties for such are high, and those roads are scary enough while you are sober. While you won't get points on your home driver's license, you may get arrested and the car impounded, which results in many costs.

Tully, Kildare

In addition to the many places already discussed above, numerous galleries and museums in Ireland are free of charge, a great way to spend a day, especially if the weather isn't great. On finer days, many parks and gardens are free as well. You often can find local festivals and fairs to shop in, listen to music, sample food, and have a grand time with little to no cost. Of course, the landscapes are free to view, as are many historical landmarks!

CHILDREN

Sometimes it is very difficult to plan trips when you have children. Whether they are young children or rebellious teenagers, finding places which have enough to keep them interested and engaged can be a challenge. There is an excellent resource I discovered through the folks of Irish Fireside, called Ireland with Kids.

WI-FI

Most hotels and many B&Bs have now started offering free Wi-Fi, though it is not always GOOD Wi-Fi, and some turn it off during the night hours. Many cafés have it, though, as will any McDonald's (not that I recommend going to McDonald's when you have so many other great options). Libraries will also have access. And, increasingly, entire towns such as Sligo, Westport, or Knock have Wi-Fi throughout.

Remember earlier when I said a trip to Ireland was less expensive than a trip to Disney? One trip to Ireland, which was eighteen days in late May, was about $2,500 per person for airfare, rental car, trip insurance, B&Bs, and food. You can spend more than this on a week in New York City, or at Disney. And there are all sorts of ways you can trim your budget even more on your trip.

The Hidden Facet—Undiscovered Places

One of the joys of traveling anywhere is finding the hidden gems, those places which are privately wonderful and probably not on the average tourist's radar. They are not likely to be in Rick Steves's guidebooks, or in the Fodor's guides.

Carrick-a-Rede Rope Bridge, Antrim

They are often found by asking a local, or another traveler, or just getting lost (deliberately or by accident) and coming across a place of wonder. There are a few 'big' tourist places thrown in, because I believe that, despite them being 'tourist traps', they are truly worth all the hype and should be seen.

The places I have found below are listed by the county in which they are located. For a map, see the end of the book in Maps and Resources. I've tried to add the official websites of each place where they exist, or if none are available, a site which includes good data on the place.

Much of my information is supplemented by Ireland Travel Kit, a fantastic resource compiled by a dedicated team of Irish travel experts and enthusiasts. This is not, by far, a comprehensive list, but just a mere taste of the list they are constantly updating. I give a special thanks to the Ireland Travel Kit contributors for giving us permission to include sites in this book.

COUNTY ANTRIM

Carrick-a-Rede Rope Bridge—This is usually listed on the 'normal' list of tourist places, but I wanted to include it anyhow. One reason is many people might give this a miss if they think it's just a little rope bridge on the coast. It is so much more. It is some of the most spectacular coastal scenery I've seen.

It is a lovely, long walk to the bridge itself, which was almost a let-down for me after the sights along the way. Go past the bridge and climb the hill a little for even more lovely views of the coast. This bridge was originally built to allow fisherman access to the island for their seasonal fishing.

Cushendall Cliff Path—This was a little difficult for us to find from the main town, but if you drive down the road the grocery store is on, you will find an entrance to Layde Church. Past the church and graveyard, you can find the coastal trail. It is well worth searching out, even on a misty, wet day, as the views of the surrounding coast are stunning.

There's a cliff path car park, but we only found this at the end of our wanderings, so I guess we did the path backwards. Part of the path is dug from the hillside, part of it has wooden walks and bridges. You can see up and down the coast, and across the ocean to Rathlin Island, or perhaps even Scotland on a clear day. Do be warned. It can be a bit treacherous in wet weather, so bring good walking shoes.

Dark Hedges—Not far from Armoy, this is the entrance to an old manor house, which has now been renovated into a resort, Gracheill Golf Club. The two centuries old entrance is lined with sensuously serpentine beech trees, forming a spooky canopy over the road, and offering a great deal of atmosphere and mystery. It is well worth a stop for a photo opportunity. It is reputed to be haunted by the Grey Lady.

The Dark Hedges, Antrim

Glenariff Forest—The Glens of Antrim is the last of Ireland's glacier valleys and today holds many delights and wonders. One of these is the Glenariff Forest, filled with primeval, mossy forests, gushing waterfalls, and sylvan splendor. There are several walks for several levels of difficulty and length.

We walked about three miles through the area and encountered about a dozen waterfalls, ranging from powerful cascades to delicate trickles. There is an area with pavilions and barbecue facilities along one trail for a nice picnic rest. We went when it was a soft, rainy, drizzly day, which just made the forest aroma stronger and the waterfalls faster. If you aren't much up for adventure, there is a large waterfall right near the entrance, with an observation deck. But please, wander in and be adventurous, it's worth it.

Layde Church—Layde Church is a small, ruined church near Cushendall. It has a delightful high cross and a keyhole cross, old and worn, as well as several other monuments and graves on a steep hill next to the sea. It's a little difficult to find, in Cushendall, turn off the main road and past the grocery store and the small park. There's a fork in the road, with a little sign, take the left fork. You can park in a small gravel lot and walk to the church.

Ballymacdermot Courth Tomb, Armagh

Narrowest House in Belfast—This small house on Great Victoria Street measures only eight feet wide. It was once a home for the church's caretaker, but doesn't have a door into the church, so qualifies as its own structure.

COUNTY ARMAGH

Ballymacdermot Court Tomb—Not far from Newry, this three-chambered court tomb can be dated between 4,000 and 2,500 BCE. It is set in a beautiful vista, offering views of the Mourne, Cooley, and Slieve Guillion mountain ranges. It was originally thought to be a Viking construction, due to some Victorian poets romanticizing the Viking invasions, conflating the terms Danann (as in Tuatha dé Danann) and Danes.

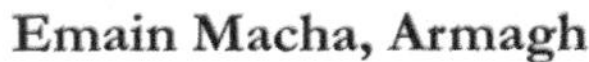

Emain Macha, Armagh

Emain Macha (Navan Fort)—Located just east of Armagh City, this is an ancient monument which, according to Celtic mythology, was a great royal site of pagan ritual. It was founded by the goddess Macha and was used as the capital of the ancient province of Ulster.

Emain Macha loosely translates to Macha's Twins and derives its name from the legend that she was the wife of a wealthy cattle owner who boasted she could run faster than the king's horses. Hearing this, the king put Macha to the test. Despite being heavily pregnant, she raced the horses and won, then delivered twins on the finish line. It was traditionally home to the warriors of the Red Branch. There is a visitor center and interactive folk park.

Moyry Castle—This square, ruined castle tower was built in 1601 by Lord Mountjoy, and stands three stories tall. It was built as a defense to the mountain gap known as the 'Gap of the North', and has unusual, rounded corners. There are no stairs inside, so you cannot climb up, but it is situated on a hill so you can enjoy views of the surrounding countryside.

COUNTY CARLOW

Adelaide Memorial Church (Miniature Salisbury Cathedral)—This church in the village of Myshall was built in 1913 by John Duguid to be a miniature copy of the Salisbury Cathedral in Wiltshire, England. It was built in memory of his daughter Constance, who was killed in a hunting accident, and her mother. In the graveyard, there is a bullaun (bowl) stone, believed to imbue healing properties to rainwater collected within it.

Rancho Reilly—This unlikely named place east of Carlow is a petting farm and children's activity centre, a great place to stop and let the kids run off some of their energy after being in the car too long, going from sacred spot to sacred spot.

COUNTY CAVAN

Giant's Leap in the Cavan Burren—The Cavan Burren is similar to the County Clare Burren, with a limestone landscape and odd rock formations. Within the Cavan Burren, there is a Wedge Tomb called Giant's Leap hidden among the trees, with five large lintel stones still in place.

There are some ring marks on the stones, dating from the Bronze Age about 4,000 years ago. There are two chambers, built with large sandstone blocks. According to legend, two giants, Lugh and Lag, both had the same lady love. To impress her, they jumped over a wide chasm, but Lag tried to do it backwards, and fell to his death. The tomb is next to that chasm.

Erica's Fairy Forest—A magical place dedicated to the memory of a young girl who died when she was six. A wonderful place for families with young children.

Killykeen Forest Park—Located near Lough Oughter, this conservation area holds a wealth of wildlife and birds. It offers canoeing, biking, and windsurfing as well as fishing.

Tullydermot Falls—A marvelous waterfall under the shadow of Cuilcagh Mountain. You can reach the falls on foot from a nearby car park.

COUNTY CLARE

Burren Perfumery—As you explore the karstic wonderland that is the Burren, take some time to stop at the Burren Perfumery. It is due east of Caherconnell, and not far from the village of Fahee. Although there's a lonely, dirt road leading to it, don't be discouraged! It's a hidden gem of scents and delight.

Within the complex, you can see how the products are made from local flora, a short film on the area, and see into the actual workshops. You can have a light meal at the cafe and relax in the shady courtyard. It reminds me of a charming villa in the French countryside, really.

Burren Smokehouse—Lisdoon, Lisdoon, Lisdoon, Lisdoonvarna! Every time I visit this area, this song is stuck in my head, the Christy Moore version, of course. Lisdoonvarna is a lovely Victorian era spa town, northeast of Doolin in County Clare. On the main road through town, the Burren Smokehouse is a marvelous place!

The shop is full of local products, from their famous smoked salmon and mackerel, as well as poitìn (Irish moonshine), mead, cheeses, teas, seaweed products, jellies, and of course, the usual course of gifts and souvenirs.

I was lucky enough to come across some storytelling CDs my first trip there, from a local man whose daughter had published his recordings. What a treasure! His name was Paddy Hynes, and he was a true bard. This is a fantastic place to load up on some breakfast and snack foods, make a picnic, and support the local community.

The Burren Perfumery

Corcomroe Abbey—We stopped by this abbey on our way out of Ballyvaughan. The early morning light and mists made this place lonelier and more mystical than I had expected. It is situated on the edge of the Burren, and the ruined arches and graves were definitely a bit eerie. It is mossy and overgrown, great for exploring.

Craggaunowen: The Living Past—If you like folk parks, you'll love this one. It offers a pre-historic site, on 50 acres of wooded grounds, with recreated homes, and artifacts such as crannogs, thatch huts, stone circles, etc. Tim Severin's Brendan Boat is housed here. And there is an area with some rare Irish animal breeds that were coming in the pre-historic era in Ireland. A crannog is a house built on a man-made island in a lake, very defensible from invaders, with a single causeway entrance.

Dysert O'Dea Cross, Clare

Dysert O'Dea Castle and High Cross—Dysert O'Dea is a simple tower castle hidden away in the rolling hills of County Clare, and worth a search. Built between 1470-1480 by Diarmaid O'Dae, Lord of the Cineal Fearmaic, this castle played an integral part in the Battle of Dysart O'Dea and the push to keep the Anglo Normans from the region.

The keep itself is open for touring and the story of the family history is interesting (the keep is back in the hands of an O'Day ancestor who bought it in 1968 and fully restored it). On the grounds you can find old cannon and other memorabilia. On the wider property of several acres, you will find twenty-five historical monuments and artifacts, including two stone forts, a *fulacht fiadh*, (ancient cooking site), the church ruin with the famous Romanesque doorway, ruined roundtower, and of course, the high crosses.

If you go back down the little road from the castle, and turn right, there is a stile (ladder/bridge) over the gate. Go carefully over this, and into the field, where you will find the lovely St. Tola's High Cross on a wide field, and many sheep to enjoy the place alongside.

Father Ted's House—Many people are fans of the Irish comedy 'Father Ted,' and if you would like a pilgrimage to the house where it was filmed, you can travel to Glenquin, near Killnaboy. This large parochial house was supposedly on the fictional Craggy Island, though it was fashioned after Inis Mór.

As this house is a private family home, it's not signposted and is not open for tours. Fans still enjoy seeing the house. To find it, in the center of Kilnaboy Village, look for the sign for Kilnaboy National School and the road sign L1112. This is a narrow country road into the hills. Turn north and drive for about five or six miles (about 10 minutes). When the road forks, stay left and continue driving. The house is a gray Georgian country house and will be on the left.

Parknabinnia Wedge Tomb—Not far from the town of Killnaboy, the area at Parknabinnia has some ten wedge tombs spread across the top of the hill. The area is easily accessible from the road. Watch for the monument sign. You will need to walk from the lay-by onto the hill. The view from the tomb is commanding so take some time to explore all around the site.

You're very likely to have it all to yourself as, unlike the nearby Poulnabrone Dolmen, you won't find busloads of tourists here. The tomb looks like it has hair, grass is growing on the large, flat capstone.

Parknabinnia Wedge Tomb, Clare

Quin Abbey—Quin Abbey is impressive, yet still charming and intimate. Originally a timber church, it was razed by Richard 'Strongbow' de Clare in 1278 and a stone keep with bawn walls and round guard towers was built in its place. In 1350, a church was built around the keep, making this site unique in Ireland.

In 1433, Franciscan monks moved in and occupied this site until the Dissolution of the Monasteries in the mid-16th century. Quin Abbey is only about nine miles from Ennis, and definitely worth a side trip to visit. I greatly enjoyed exploring this ruin and the surrounding grounds. It was filled with soaring arches and dancing shadows from the late afternoon sun.

COUNTY CORK

An Shrone—This site is rather difficult to get to, making it a VERY hidden gem. About 3 km (under 2 miles) from the town of Rathmore in north County Cork, you will see the sign for Shrone. Drive up this road to the crossroads and you will see a sign for The City points you up a very narrow path to this site, which you are advised to walk to.

The Irish '*Cromlech Cathair Croabh Dearg*' translates to the Fort of the Red Claw. It has been a site of pagan worship since ancient times, as it was sacred to Dana, Mother of the Gods and thought to be one of the first places of settlement in Ireland. There is a holy well, and a once large stone circle and beehive huts. Today, The City still attracts worshipers who come to pray for healthy herds and bountiful crops.

Quin Abbey, Clare

Ballycrovane Ogham Stone—Ballycrovane Ogham stone is impressive, rising seventeen feet up out of a hill on the edge of the Ring of Beara. It has, carved along one side, Ogham marked into it. Ogham is the ancient Celtic language, largely used for ceremonial purposes, and the only known written language of the pre-Roman Celts. We came across it by accident, thanks to a lovely little brown sign and a curiosity not deterred by the fact we had to go up some farmer's driveway, through his gate, and into what was essentially his backyard to find it. But find it we did, and it was suitably impressive.

Blackrock Castle Observatory—Built into a former guard tower on the harbor in Cork City, the observatory is a wonderful place to visit. During the day, the museum is open to visitors, as is the on-site café. Tours of the famous dungeons are given on the weekends. Fancy a look at the stars from Ireland's shore? Stop by this place on First Fridays, the first Friday of every month, for a free and fun night gazing into the heavens.

Derreenataggart Stone Circle—Located near Castletownbere, this recumbent stone circle is located on a farm up an out of the way winding and twisty one-lane road. There is a small parking area nearby, and a lovely vista of mountains in the distance.

Derreenataggart Stone Circle, Cork

Drombeg Stone Circle—Also known as the Druid's Altar, this is a large stone circle in excellent shape, built a couple kilometers east of Glandore. It has some cup marks and is oriented for the winter solstice. There is a *fulacht fiadh,* or cooking pit, that may have been in use as late as the 600s. Come early or late in the day to avoid crowds, and don't miss the small hut near the cooking pit.

Gougane Barra, Cork

Eyeries—This is a lovely, charming town along the Ring of Beara which shines with brightly colored houses and an old-world, frozen in time feel. The town is the result of workers living in the region when copper mining was an active industry. Today, this is a thriving community with lively pubs with traditional music and dancing, and friendly folk to have a pint with. Great hikes and walks in the surrounding hills and mountains will take you into the mining areas.

There's a tiny church called St. Kentigern Church overlooking the bay. And don't miss Ballycrovane Ogham stone, the tallest in Ireland, recorded at 17.5 feet (5.3 m) high. It bears the inscription 'MAQI DECCEDDAS AVI TURANIAS' which translates as 'Mac Deich Uí Turainn' or 'son of Deich, the descendant of Turainn'. Neither of these two people is known in Irish history.

Gougane Barra—*Guagán Barra, meaning Finbarr's Hollow*, is Ireland's first forest park in the heart of south County Cork and surrounded by the Sheehy Mountains, and is a lovely photo spot and a great place for walking trails and a small waterfall.

On Holy Island, a small island in the middle of the lake, you will find a small Romanesque-style chapel beside the 6th-century monastic settlement which still retains the original priests' cells. There is a narrow bridge onto Holy Island. At the gate, you'll find St. Finbarr's Holy Well dedicated to the founder of Cork City.

There's also a graveyard containing some local legends, Tailor and Antsy (Timothy and Anastasia Buckley). He was a *seanachai* (storyteller) and conversationalist. His biography was banned due to a bit of raciness.

Ring of Beara, Cork

Ring of Beara—While this is a rather large place to be considered 'hidden', it is often overlooked in the shadow of the Dingle and Iveragh peninsulas. The Beara Peninsula is considered the jewel in Ireland's crown. The roads are a little too narrow for the tour buses, which means the crowds are smaller, but the tourist amenities are fewer, as well.

It will take a good day to explore the peninsula, but even a misty day is spectacular. Rocky areas full of shale from old mines which make the region look like a moonscape are interspersed with charming, bright-painted towns strung along like rainbow pearls. Drive slowly and carefully, and enjoy things like Healy Pass, Dursey Island and Cable Car, and other areas to get out and explore.

St. Gobnait's Well—Known as Gobnait of the bees, this well and house in Ballyvourney is dedicated to St. Gobnait, a 6th century saint who may have been associated with a legend which tells how she was known to set bees on invaders to the village.

In the 1950s, a tall stone statue was erected to her honor near her settlement. There is a set of holy stations you can see, a sheela-na-gig, portal stones and a holy well. Driving west on the N22, turn left just after the Abbey Hotel and follow the signs for the church and graveyard.

COUNTY DONEGAL

Ardara—The beach near Ardara features a very long inlet with villages all along it and a wonderful rock outcropping which gets slammed by the waves on a windy day. On the other side of the inlet are the Eos Waterfall and Maghera Sea Caves, with a surreal exploration into seven-foot-tall sand dunes to find them. Ardara is a small town on the west coast of County Donegal. It is a very walkable, friendly place, with great pubs and stunning sites nearby.

Donagh Cross—Carndonagh is a town on the Inishowen 100 driving route and well worth a visit if you are at all interested in Celtic High Crosses. We came across this place by accident, and I was thrilled to find the 7th century Donagh Celtic Cross, also known as St. Patrick's Cross. It has two pillars, one on either side, with carved Celtic knotwork faces on them, strangely reminiscent of the faces on the Isle of Lewis chess pieces found in Scotland.

Glencolmcille, Donegal

Glencolmcille Folk Village—The lovely Glencolmcille Folk Village, aka Father McDyer's Folk Village Museum, is the recreation of a replica of a small thatch village that was typical in the 18th, 19th, and early 20th centuries. Each cottage (all with thatched roofs, of course) has furniture, tools, and décor typical of the era they represent. There is a small gift shop with local crafts, and a cafe to stop at and enjoy.

This village is set in one of Ireland's *gaeltachts*, Irish speaking regions, and overlooks Glen Bay Beach. Further up the road, there is a pilgrimage with stations which you can follow, and a stunning view across the sea cliffs.

Grianan of Ailleach—*Grianán Ailigh*, also known as the Temple of the Sun, is a Bronze Age fort, may have been built around 500-600 CE, or perhaps even farther back, and commands a spectacular view of the surrounding countryside. It's not a particularly tall hill, but it's taller than anything nearby.

You can see north over the Inishowen Peninsula. The fort is in good repair, and you can climb up steps built into the walls to the top of the fort. It was the ancient seat of the Ui Neill clan for many centuries.

The drive up to the fort is a bit harrowing, with single track roads and very high hedges. However, there's a decent-sized parking area near the top, and the rest of the distance is a short climb. It has boards for maintenance vehicles to drive up, and you could probably get a wheelchair up with some effort. It is very close to Derry City, and an easy trip from many places in County Donegal. It would make a wonderful stop on the way to or from the Inishowen Peninsula.

Ardara, Donegal

Inishowen 100—The *Inis Eoghain* 100 (Inishowen) is a 100-mile-long scenic drive around the Inishowen Peninsula in

County Donegal. It is a lovely day trip, showing beaches, sea cliffs, charming towns, and all sorts of Irish delights. Technically, it starts in Bridgend, but you can start wherever you wish.

Fanad Lighthouse

Don't miss delights such as Kinnagoe Bay, a serene sandy beach surrounded by rocky cliffs, or the Wee House of Malin, an ancient ruined monastic church site on a rocky point. There are thatched cottages dotted here and there, of course. Do be careful, our TomTom GPS unit sent us up over a mountain on a sheep track. While visiting Malin town, why not journey up to Malin Head, which is the most northerly point on the island of Ireland (opposite is Mizen Head in Southwest Cork).

Kilclooney Dolmen—Just northwest of Ardara, take a twenty-minute drive to Kilclooney Beg. Park near St. Conal's church (there is a dolmen centre), there is a small farmhouse nearby, the dolmen is in the bog lands behind the farmhouse. Be sure to wear shoes which will stand up to boggy conditions! Please stay to the right and close the gate behind you.

Kilclooney Dolmen, Donegal

Go through the gate, and about ten minutes of walking will get you there. As close as it is to a village, the peat fields around the dolmen make it isolated and lonely, very primeval. You can't get right up to it, there are ditches dug around it to prevent this. However, it is nonetheless very impressive, and dates from about 3,500 BCE. There is a second, smaller dolmen behind the first.

Kinnagoe Bay—Kinnagoe Beach, near Mossy Glen in the Inishowen Peninsula, is a spectacular beach, and well isolated from the teeming tourist crowds. Its soft, sandy beach is a haven from the rocky outcroppings, and you can see for miles over the sea into the distance. One of the ships of the Spanish Armada, the Trinidad Valencera, sank off the coast here in 1588.

Mount Errigal—Errigal Mountain dominates the landscape in this area and is the tallest peak in the county. It is a fairly hikeable mountain, with a 'one-man's pass' along the top.

However, you will need proper gear, good shoes, a walking stick, etc.

If you want advice or assistance, you could go by (or stay at!) the Errigal Hostel, just down the road from the car park you should start at for the climb. Errigal Hostel has recently obtained 'green' status by the EU. They can lead treks up the mountain fairly frequently and are very helpful to those wanting to make the journey. The surrounding countryside is sublime, even if you don't climb. Errigal is at one end of the Seven Sisters, and nearby the Bloody Foreland.

St. Columba's Well—If you drive to the other side of the bay from the Glencolmcille Folk Village, and walk up the promontory, you can find St. Colmcille's Holy Well and the other holy stations associated with St. Colmcille and his journeys. Even if you aren't interested in the spirituality of the location, the views are spectacular.

COUNTY DOWN

Ards Peninsula—This arm of land which cradles Strangford Lough from the Irish Sea has many towns and villages strung along it, a mild marine climate, and much wildlife. Sites such as Scrabo Tower, Mount Stewart House and Gardens, Millisle seaside village and amusement park, Portavogie with traditional fishing boats and fresh seafood run along it. You can take the ferry between Strangford town and Portaferry if you only have time for part of the peninsula.

Castle Ward—This castle looks more like a palace or manor house, built in the 18th century by Bernard Ward, the 1st Viscount Bangor. They could not agree on style (Palladian vs. Gothic), so they split the house in half, with one Palladian façade and one Gothic façade. There is an extensive estate with gardens, walking trails, mills, shops, and a fortified tower house. The castle is near the town of Strangford.

Nendrum Monastic Site—Dating from the 5th century, it has links to St. Patrick and consists of three nested dry-stone walls, a central church ruin, and sundial, with the remains of a round tower and graveyard. Find this site near the town of Comber.

Old Castle Ward, Down

COUNTY DUBLIN

Ballybrack Dolmen—To prove that you can expect to find interesting things in unassuming places, situated in the suburbs of Dublin on a residential green, you can visit the Ballybrack Dolmen.

Bookshops—Dublin has many hidden bookshops, many of them with both new and used books, great for those that love to browse, find hidden written treasures, or just like to relax with a good book on a rainy afternoon in the city. The childhood home of George Bernard Shaw on 33 Synge Street is one such place, as is Hodges Figgis on Dawson Street, especially for books on Irish topics.

Books Upstairs on College Green has a collection of new and hard to find books. Chapters on Mid. Abbey Street has a huge selection of used books, as does the Winding Stair Bookshop on Lower Ormond Quay.

Christ Church Cathedral—This cathedral dates back to pre-Norman times when the timber church was razed and the stone one went up in its place, courtesy of private funds from Bishop Laurence O'Toole (now St. Laurence) and Richard 'Strongbow' de Clare, a Norman Nobleman who married the King of Leinster's only daughter, Aoife.

Christ Church boasts the largest open crypts in Europe, stunning architecture and history, and the mummified remains of a cat and rat! During the cleaning of one of the organs in storage, a cat and rat were found in one of the pipes, the cat probably having chased the rat into the pipe and both getting stuck. The pair have been put into a protective case and put on display. The church also has an effigy of Strongbow.

Cú Chulainn Statue—The General Post Office (GPO) is on most Dublin Tour highlights due to its role in the 1916 rising, but inside the Mail Hall, there is a lovely bronze statue of the legendary Irish hero, Cú Chulainn. The statue is a memorial to those that participated in the Rising and depicts the hero facing his enemies even in death, having tied himself to a pillar.

Dun Laoghaire—Pronounced Dun Leery, this is a lovely seaside town on the outskirts of Dublin which makes a nice base to explore the area. Dun Laoghaire is Ireland's oldest established town, earning its charter in 498CE.

The town name was changed to Kingstown in Georgian times but saw the name reverted during the time of the Irish Free State. Getting its start as a harbor town, Dun Laoghaire still remains the hub of sea travel, with ferries to England and Wales, the National Yacht Club, and twin piers which protect an active inner harbor.

There are lovely views out to see and to the Howth Peninsula across Dublin Bay. There are many things to do in and near Dun Laoghaire, including the Sunday Market in The People's Park, Joyce Tower, and the National Maritime Museum.

Glasthule Village melds into Dun Laoghaire where you will find Bullock Castle. Stay on this road for Dalkey, a town famous for not just the seven castles, but also for being Ireland's Beverly Hills. The DART commuter train runs along the eastern coast between Greystones, County Wicklow and Howth in North County Dublin, with three stops in Dublin City, making this an ideal location to explore the area from.

Glasnevin Cemetery—The first grave at Glasnevin Cemetery, aka Prospect Cemetery, was dug in 1832. Until this time, Catholics never had a graveyard of their own, due too repressive Penal Laws. Today the cemetery is the largest in Ireland, encompassing 124 acres and over one million interments.

Glasnevin offers a fascinating view into the changing style of burial monuments of nearly two centuries, from the austere to classic High Cross to nationalistic revival. In an effort to deter body snatchers, 'Sack-em-ups' or 'resurrectionists,'

Glasnevin was surrounded by high medieval style walls with ten watchtowers overlooking the grounds and surrounding area.

Armed night watchmen were hired, who became known as 'Charlies.' Some of Ireland's most famous and most notorious are buried here: politicians, activists, and rebels, to artists, writers, and musicians, etc. Take an organized tour or get a map from the visitor's center and wander on your own. When you reach the original entrance to the site, take a moment to step through the gates and into John Kavanagh's Pub, better known as the Gravedigger's Pub. The pub was established in 1833 and has not been refurbished since, with the exception of some dim lighting.

Iveagh Gardens—(pronounced Ivy), these gardens can be found behind the National Concert Hall in Dublin City near St. Stephen's Green. They were created in 1863 by Sir Benjamin Lee Guinness, 1st Baronette, son of Sir Arthur Guinness of the Guinness Brewery Guinness's. The style of these gardens is partway between 'French Formal' and 'English Landscape' style. They include a rustic grotto, a cascade, sunken formal panels of lawn, archery grounds, and rockeries.

Malahide—Malahide is a coastal town, ten miles north of Dublin, with a fantastic active fishing community since Viking times. There was once a monastic settlement here; St. Sylvester's Well can still be visited on Old Street. The main draw to this town is Malahide Castle, the grounds of which include restored gardens and the Model Rail Village for train enthusiast. Malahide is serviced by DART, with a connection at Connelly Station in Dublin City.

Marsh's Library—While the Old Library in Trinity College is gorgeous, and on most 'must see' lists of Dublin, another lovely old library is Marsh's, just up the Cathedral Close from St. Patrick's Cathedral. It is close to its original condition and won't be as crowded as the more famous cousin in Trinity.

The Viking Experience—While this isn't exactly a hidden gem, it does have some fascinating aspects that make it worth a visit. The information offered in the Synod Hall and Dublinia is quite interesting, and it's near the last remaining piece of Dublin City's original city walls, as well as Ireland's oldest church, St. Audoen's.

Boa Island, Fermanagh

COUNTY FERMANAGH

Boa Island—This island near Lough Erne is about five miles long, but very narrow. There is a road bridge onto the island, so no ferry is necessary. There are raths, carved stones, and a cairn. The main feature of Boa Island is the Caldragh Cemetery near Pettigo. Little is known about this cemetery, but it has been dated to the early Irish Christian period (400-800CE).

Tucked in an enclosure of trees, this cemetery contains little more than stone markers for those buried here. What makes this graveyard remarkable are two hand carved anthropomorphic stone statues called the Boa Island Figure, aka the Janus Stone, and the Lustymore Island Figure. These carvings are either pre- or early Christian creations or may date from the Iron Age.

Castle Saunderson—Once the seat of the Saunderson family from the 16th century Plantation period, the house has seen a number of uses, including a hotel but was damaged by fire, the third to occur in the castle, and never refurbished. The house was eventually sold to Scouting Ireland in 1997. President Michael D. Higgins unveiled the €3.7 million European-funded Castle Saunderson International Scouting Centre in Cavan on 18 August 2012. Castle Saunderson is on the Cavan/Fermanagh border near the town of Belturbet, Co. Cavan.

Marble Arch Caves Global Geopark—Formed 650 million years ago, underground rivers meander through the mountains. You can take a boat ride on through the caverns to see the stalagmites and stalactites, as well as The Castle gour pool, a natural rimstone pool and the largest in these caves. Legends of Fionn Mac Cumhaill are associated with this area, as well as the Tuatha dé Danann.

COUNTY GALWAY

Aran Islands, Galway

The Aran Islands consist of three Islands—Inis Oirr, Inis Man, and Inis Mór. These listings are for Inis Mór, the big island.

Man of Aran Cottage—Back in 1931, there was a film made called the Man of Aran. It was about a fisherman's life on the island, and a wonderful snapshot into the way of life at the time in this rustic place. This B&B cottage was created out of other cottages for this film and is conveniently located near the hamlet of Eóghanacht, and the stunning cliff fort of Dún Aengosa.

Inis Mór

Seal Colony on Inis Mór—As you drive, walk, or ride your bikes along the road from Kilronan to the hamlet of Eóghanacht, there is a fork in the road, head towards the coast, to the right. As you go along this road, you will see several lengths of beach, one of them called Portmurvy. Look closely!

There are likely seals sunning themselves on the rocks below. Did that rock move? Yes! It's a seal. At first, we didn't see any of the seals move. We had the uncharitable thought perhaps they were just statues, put there to fool the tourists, and then one started flipping his tail at us, and we knew they were, indeed, real.

Seven Churches—*Na Seacht dTeampaill* in Irish, is a ruin of several ancient churches on the island. The site is near the middle of the island and can be reached in many ways from the main port town of Kilronan. It's about five miles in, and a lovely long walk or bike ride. Alternatively, you can hire one of the many pony and traps or taxis which ferry tourists around the sites on the island. It's a short distance past the Man of Aran Cottage and *Dún Aonghasa* (Dun Aengus).

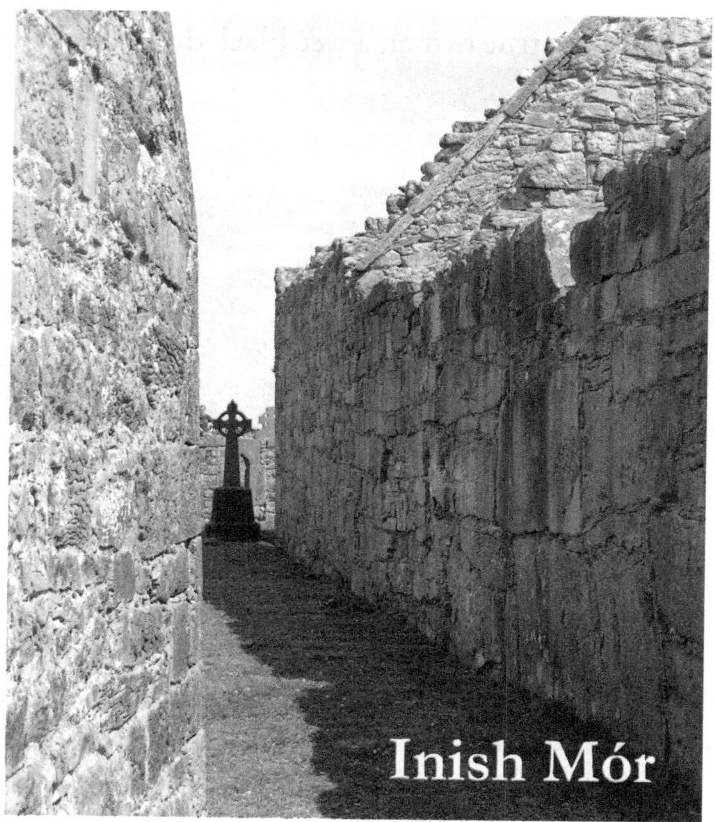

Tí Joe Watty's Pub- If you spend some time on *Inis Mór* (and I mean more than the couple of hours which a day trip encompasses), please take some time to visit Joe Watty's Pub. Many nights have music, and the place gets pumping with drinks and dancing, though some nights are quieter. We've visited on a Saturday night, and the music was grand, the crowds were thick, and the buzz was high. And we've been there on a Sunday evening, after the day trippers and weekenders had gone home, when it was quieter.

The Aran Islands are one of Ireland's *gaeltachts* (Irish speaking region) so most of the conversations I heard around me were in Irish, and the owner came over for a lovely chat. Not only do they have fantastic food (the mackerel salad is divine!), but the owners and staff truly care about the hospitality of the place, and the island. This pub is on the edge of Kilronan, on the main road out of town, you can't miss it. Don't forget to stop and say hello to the true owner, a wee black dog called Guinness.

Inis Oirr

Coole Park—Once the home of Lady Augusta Gregory, all that remains of the once grand estate today is the stable, now serving as a tearoom, and the original walled garden. Lady Gregory was instrumental in writing down the oral histories of the servants and tenants on her land, thus preserving them for future generations. She and close friend, William Butler Yeats, created a community of writers who came to Coole house for relaxation, creativity, and other literary pursuits.

This group of literary enthusiasts included dramatist, George Bernard Shaw; poet, John Masefield; first President of Ireland, Douglas Hyde; playwright, Sean O'Casey; artist, writer, and brother to WB Yeats, Jack B Yeats; among others, including Elinor Monsell who designed Dublin's Abbey Theatre's logo which is still in use today. This group founded the Abbey Theatre, and they were instrumental in preserving Irish literature during a time called the Irish Literary Revival.

Each of the members of this community carved their initials into the trunk of a young Copper Beech Tree, which is now the main attraction in the old walled garden. The Autograph

Tree is now behind protective high fencing for the protection of the tree.

The estate grounds are now mostly left to nature and open to the public and full of trails to follow through the woods and along the banks of Coole Lough. Near Gort, you will find the Lady Gregory Museum, and further along is the turn off for WB Yeats' famous Yeats' Tower, aka Thoor Ballylee, where Yeats wrote his famous story, The Tower.

Kilmacduagh Monastery—About 5 km from Gort, this monastery has the tallest roundtower in Ireland (30 meters), nicknamed the Leaning Tower of Kilmacduagh. There are several smaller church and castle ruins on the site, and well worth an exploration. The site was founded on legend, as Saint Colman MacDaugh was supposedly walking through the woods when his girdle fell to the ground, prompting him to build the monastery there. It is also said that no man of the diocese will die from lightning.

Portumna Castle—A stately manor house open to the public, this semi-fortified house includes geometric gardens, with fruit trees, flowers, herbs, and vegetables. It is near Lough Derg and the River Shannon as well as Portumna Forest Park. It is considered the height of elegance and taste, at least it was by its builder, Richard Burke, 4th Earl of Clanricarde. It houses a museum for the Flight of the Wild Geese, which refers to the departure of the Irish Jacobite army after the Williamite War in Ireland, circa 1691.

COUNTY KERRY

Ardfert Cathedral—We came across this cathedral on our way from Ballyvaughan to Dingle one day. Once off the Shannon Ferry in Tarbert, we took the coastal road toward Dingle and stopped in Ardfert. The cathedral was built in the 12th century on the site of a 6th century settlement founded by

St. Brendan, aka St. Brendan the Navigator. It fell into ruin in 1641 during the Irish Rebellion.

While it is an extensive ruin, you will be treated to some lovely architecture, including lovely colonnades and Romanesque doorways and windows, blind arcading, ecclesiastical effigies, etc. There is a carving of a wyvern in one of the windows, and there are grotesques and Celtic crosses here and there. It is on a busy street, so there lacks the quiet solitude of some of the better situated abbeys, but it is worth a visit.

Carrigafoyle Castle, Kerry

Carrigafoyle Castle—Built in the 1490s by Conor Liath O'Connor-Kerry, Carrigafoyle (Carraig an Phoill in Irish means 'rock of the hole') was considered one of the strongest of Irish fortresses if its time. This is a large tower house which is common across the north of the Munster province. It stands on the rock shore in a small bay off the Shannon estuary near Ballylongford, County Kerry.

The castle was once called the guardian of the Shannon because of its strategic position overlooking the river which was a once active shipping lane that supplied goods to Limerick City. The castle fell in battle in the famous Siege of Carrigafoyle Castle at Easter in 1580. Today the keep stands sentinel to a past time.

Celtic and Prehistoric Museum—This museum is located on the Dingle Peninsula near Ventry. This small, privately owned museum has a surprising wealth of ancient artifacts, from fossilized bones to Celtic tools and jewelry. The museum also has Ireland's only fully intact Wooly Mammoth skull, as well as the only complete baby dinosaur skeleton, a large nest of dinosaur eggs, and a Cave Bear skeleton. The owner is an American ex-pat who is passionate about his collection and makes a lovely host. He has local wares for sale in his shop.

Puck the Goat Fair—The Puck Fair *(Aonach an Phuic)* is Ireland's oldest festival, and one legend says its origins come from a Billy goat, or 'puck,' which was separated from his herd when Cromwellian forces were approaching the area. The appearance of the exhausted animal alerted villages and they were able to protect themselves from attack. Every year a group of people go up into the mountains and catch a wild goat.

The goat is brought back to the town for the crowning ceremony. Traditionally, a young schoolgirl from one of the local primary schools is crowned 'Queen of the Puck' and it's she who crowns the goat 'King Puck.' The goat is then put into a small cage on a high stand in the middle of the town square and remains there for the duration of the festival. Of course, he's treated well and brought down at night. Pubs are allowed to stay open until 3am, which is an exception in that pubs in Ireland are required to be closed by midnight most nights, 11pm on Sunday.

The fair includes the usual food and music, craft stalls and family activities. Also occurring at this time is the famous Kilorglin Horse Fair takes place on the 10th, and on the 11th is the Kilorglin Cattle Fair.

Riasc Monastic Settlement—Located on the Dingle Peninsula, this extensive site has several *clochāns*, or dry-stone huts, which are the remains of a 6th century monastic site. It is not far from the Gallarus Oratory, and has its own square oratory, or small church. There is the Riasc Stone, decorated with spiral Celtic designs. Both Riasc Monastic Settlement and Gallarus Oratory are well signposted on the Slea Head Drive near Ballyferriter.

Skellig Michael—(*Sceilig Mhichíl*) is the collective name for islands off the south Kerry coast. The Great Skellig (*Sceilig Mhór*) is the largest of the islands and which was inhabited by the greater community of monks who founded a monastery here sometime between the 6th and 8th centuries in a place considered the edge of the World.

It was occupied into the 12th century, being abandoned for no apparent reason. This site today is on the UNESCO World Heritage List. 13 boat licenses are granted each year to tour operators who are allowed to make one trip to the islands per day in the summer (April through October), weather permitting.

For safety reasons, the islands are closed in inclement weather due to falling rocks on the islands.

There are also dive sites around the islands which can be accessed by private boats, but access onto the islands is prohibited. While this site is not exactly hidden, it is a bit more difficult to get to. I have tried three times to get there, each time foiled by the weather. I will get there, though! There are thousands of sea birds, including adorable puffins, flying around the islands, and some incredible scenery.

Access has been limited in recent years due to popularity after filming for Star Wars on the island.

Staigue Stone Fort, Kerry

Staigue Fort—Located on the Ring of Kerry near Caherdaniel, this extensive fort is well worth the slow, narrow road into its demesne. It is huge, thick, strong walls which are climbable, and command a view of the ocean, miles away. This would be a perfectly defensible spot for any Celtic chieftain.

Uragh Stone Circle—This circle is located inside Gleninchaquin Park in the village of Tuosist on the Kerry side of the Beara Peninsula. It is well worth the trek up the stony, narrow road through the park for the view, even if you are uninterested in stone circles. This stone circle is dramatically situated on a spit of land which reaches out into Cloonee Lough. You can see the entire valley around you and a waterfall on the far side of the glen. There is a courtesy box which asks for a donation for upkeep of the site near the car park.

Uragh Stone Circle

COUNTY KILDARE

Curragh Plains—aka The Curragh of Kildare. While it may seem strange to include almost 50,000 acres of grassland as a 'hidden place', it is unique, as it is perhaps the oldest and largest tract of natural grassland in Europe, having been in its current state for thousands of years. It has several archeological sites and was traditionally a place where ancient Irish royals raced their horses. Today, Curragh Camp is where the Irish Army train.

The Curragh Racecourse is the largest and most famous in the country. The Curragh Plains played an instrumental function in the Easter Rebellion of 1916. Wandering the hills, you will find dugout trenches under large gorse shrubs which were used by soldiers hiding from British troops. Also, you will find rows of dugout latrines, cannon and gun huts, and practice ranges. The gently rolling hills are popular for walkers and hikers, or you can take a round of golf at the Curragh Golf Course. At the Junction 12 roundabout for Newbridge, take a moment to see the Fionn Mac Cumhaill monument which was erected in 2010 to honor the one-time Curragh home of this legendary hero at *Dún Ailinne.*

Dún Ailinne—Not to be confused with the Hill of Allen (Cnoc Alúine), this is an ancient ceremonial site dating back to around 300BCE and located on the hill of Cnoc Ailinne (Knockaulin) near Kilcullen behind the Curragh. According to Irish mythology, Dún Ailinne was one of the great royal sites of early Gaelic Ireland and is believed to have been where the Kings of Leinster were inaugurated, and home to the warrior band, the Fianna.

It's similar to the other royal sites of Tara (Kings of Meath), Navan Fort (Kings of Ulster) and Rathcroghan (Kings of Connacht). There is now an interpretative site in Nicholastown, a townland just south of Kilcullen, featuring a small-scale reproduction of what the mound may have looked like in its time.

Maynooth Castle—This ruin is the entrance to the South Campus of the National University of Ireland. The castle was built in the 12th century by the Fitzgerald family who occupied this region until the 17th century when it suffered destruction in two major wars—first during the Eleven Years War, aka The Confederate War (1641 and 1653), and then the Cromwellian War (1649-1953).

The Fitzgeralds left Maynooth after Cromwell's siege and the castle fell into disrepair, though some restoration was restarted in 2000 to allow visitors a safe visit. Be sure to stroll around the university, too. This school is the main educational institution for training men to enter the priesthood. The church has wonderful stained glass and stone hand carvings. There is a small and very old apple orchard in the back, and over the stone wall a lovely cottage garden.

St Brigid, Kildare

St. Brigid's Well, Kildare—St. Brigid is one of the three patron saints of Ireland, and has dozens of holy wells dedicated to her throughout the island. Echoes of the Goddess Brigid are heard in the saint's stories, and some of the wells, like this one, have a clootie tree, a wishing tree, nearby. The well itself has a statue of Brigit holding a flame, as she is dedicated to fire, the hearth, and smith-crafting, as well as poetry.

One is meant to tie a piece of cloth to the tree while making a wish. As the cloth deteriorates, the wish is released into the air. Nearby you can visit the Irish National Stud and Japanese Gardens, which also includes the above-mentioned St. Fiacre's Garden.

This makes for a lovely afternoon of wandering, especially in foaling season, March through May, as the mares and foals will be in the paddocks stretching their legs. Kildare is only a short drive from Dublin and would make a nice day trip from the city.

Straffan Butterfly Farm—For a lovely day of flowers and butterflies, explore the farm and exhibition. This is a great kids' activity, and an opportunity to sit and relax, taking in the Irish beauty which surrounds you. The interpretive center includes displays of unusual insects, spiders, snakes, and more. The small theater offers a glimpse into the life of butterflies and natural flora and fauna to Ireland. The Butterfly House is lush with greenery and thick with butterflies from around the world. Out in their own gardens you'll see many of Ireland's native species. This is a fun place to bring the kids.

COUNTY KILKENNY

Black Abbey—This is one of several religious sites in the medieval city of Kilkenny and is a lovely place to visit. It was established in the 13th century and is today a Catholic Dominican Priory. It has a lovely Rosary Window and a very organic, modern stained glass representing the holy flame.

The Black Abbey was established in 1225 by William Marshall, son-in-law of Richard 'Strongbow' de Clare, as one of the first houses of the Dominican Order in Ireland. The name Black Abbey comes from the Dominicans who were often referred to as 'Black Friars' on account of the black cappa or cloak which they wear over their white habits.

The abbey has had a long and tumultuous history, including suffering through the Black Death, deposition by Queen Elizabeth I, national wars, reclamation of the abbey, and eventual re-consecration, operating today as an active church for Kilkenny locals.

Inistioge Village—If you have ever seen the movie Circle of Friends, based on the book written by Irish author Maeve Binchy, you have seen Inistioge, a lovely village centered on a square, and surrounded by the rolling hills of County Kilkenny. Nearby, the beautiful ten-arched stone bridge over the River Nore which was built in 1763 on the site of an earlier bridge. Visit some of the shops used in much of the film. Have a short lunch break at the Circle of Friends Pub for a great meal.

Jerpoint Abbey—I have visited this wonderful abbey three times now and love the feel of the place. Founded in the 12th century by Benedictine monks, and then taken over by the Cistercians, the abbey was fully self-contained, including gardens producing food for the monks, an infirmary, granary, and stables, among other outbuildings.

It has a wonderful arcade of carvings along one passage, with snakes, kings and queens on each pillar. History tells us that knights on pilgrimage to the Holy Land during the Crusades 'rescued' the bones of St. Nicholas and brought them to Ireland. They are reputed to be resting somewhere within the church walls at Jerpoint. Every December, locals host a Christmas celebration in the abbey to honor St. Nicholas. Yes, THAT St. Nicholas, which is actually where my last name comes from.

Kells Priory, Kilkenny

Kells Priory—Kells Priory is one of the largest and most impressive medieval monastic settlements in Ireland, second only to Glendalough in the Wicklow Mountains which is a much earlier site. Set on the shores of King's River, this Augustine priory retains its walls and guard towers surrounding the abbey and immediate grounds, taking in a little more than three acres in total.

This gives the priory the appearance of being a fortress more than a place of worship, however this is expected, as this was a very important, and rich, religious site in its day. It has tall medieval towers which strike up against the landscape of the low rolling hills and has been called the 'Seven Castles' as a result.

Excavations carried out between 1972 and 1993 revealed more than twenty thousand artifacts: pottery, floor and ridge tiles, carved stones, metal objects, and painted window glass which has allowed the reconstruction of what some of the original windows may have looked like. This extensive ruin is well worth exploring.

Kenny's Well—He goes by several names—Kenny, Cainnech, Canice, Canicus, Kenneth. The 6th century saint even lends his moniker to the city of Kilkenny (*Cill Chainnigh*, meaning 'church of Cainnech,' or Kenny).

Kenny's Well is a short walk from the city centre and protected by a stone 'house' has been built around it. A trough, or gully, directs the holy water into the nearby river. Tradition has it that those leaving Ireland should drink from the well before they depart, though this is not recommended today.

The waters were also thought to offer protection from illness and religious faith. The waters also assured of a happy return to Ireland. This well is also said to have been the baptismal side of the last great pagan king, King Brude. Canice is said to be one of the original twelve apostles of Ireland sent out under the blessing of Saint Finnian.

Kilfane—Near Inistioge is the village of Kilfane. Here you will find the ruins of the 13th century Kilfane Church, which have traces of the original consecration crosses, the ogee-headed doorways, remains of the altar, sedelia, and book rest. On the north wall inside the church is the effigy of a Norman knight in full armor. It is referred to as Cantwell Fada, aka The Long Man. This effigy is the tallest of its kind in Ireland, or Britain. Also here is Kilfane House, the seat of the Power family who were responsible for creating Kilfane Glen and Waterfall, a romantic era garden and waterfall.

Kilmogue Portal Tomb—This portal tomb is known locally as *'Leac na Scail',* which means Stone of the Warrior. It is situated near Harristown in South Co. Kilkenny, Ireland. It is the tallest dolmen in Ireland, standing eighteen feet at the top of the capstone; the tallest portal stone is fourteen feet tall. The sill between them is nearly as high, blocking the entrance. This tomb is spectacular and well worth the drive to see it.

Kyteler's Inn—Kilkenny is a medieval town and, as such, has many little alleys or 'slipways' with cobblestone streets and hidden passages between buildings. On one such, just near Kilkenny Castle, you will find Kyteler's Inn. The place is named after Dame Alice de Kyteler, a local resident who was tried for witchcraft in the 13th century. She escaped and disappeared without a trace, but her servant girl and son were caught and tried in her place. We went there for a lovely night of Irish Traditional music and enjoyed the medieval décor and atmosphere.

Rothe House, Kilkenny

Rothe House—In the heart of the medieval city of Kilkenny, what would be a better site for a medieval merchant's museum? Rothe House was built around 1600 CE and was the home of a merchant called John Rothe Fitz-Piers. This townhouse is actually made up of three houses, three enclosed courtyards, and a large, reconstructed garden with an orchard. It was turned into a slice of life at the time. Today, the gardens have been restored and part of the house contains a museum with some local genealogy data. It is open to the public displaying some 2,500 artifacts.

COUNTY LAOIS

Heywood Gardens—Heywood House was originally built here in the late 18th century by Frederick Trench. Typically, manor houses also supported an immaculate garden. While the house has been converted into the local school, the gardens remain open to the public and are a definite must see.

Wander through the high hedges from the parking area and the walled garden suddenly appears. Set on the edge of a hillside, views beyond the estate can be seen over the walls and through porthole style openings within the wall. The focal point of this sunken garden are oval terraces which decent to a stunning elliptical fountain.

The terraces are landscaped with colorful plants and flowers, the walls covered in vines in places. At the back on the top level is a loggia, an architectural feature which is not a folly, roofed with red tiles and includes many hand-carved stone figures with inscriptions taken from the writings of Alexander Pope, a popular poet at the time. This site is well signposted from the town of Abbeyleix.

Rock of Dunamase—The Rock of Dunamase (*Dún Másc*, meaning 'the fort of Másc') is one of the most historic sites in Ireland. The castle was built in the late 12th century, most likely by Richard 'Strongbow' de Clare who was given the land by his father-in-law, Dermot MacMurrough, as a wedding gift on marrying Aoife.

This site was on the northwestern edge of the Leinster province, ruled by Kind MacMurrough. The keep was erected here to protect provincial boundaries. The lands then passed into the hands when de Clare's daughter married William Marshall who was known in his day as the greatest knight in England.

Today visitors can wander the ruins, which overlook surrounding countryside, offering stunning views of patchwork fields. This site is loosely signposted along the motorway around the town of Portlaoise (port-leesh).

Timahoe Round Tower—This 12th century roundtower is one of many that dot the Irish countryside. It's not the tallest, nor does it have as rich a history as some. What it does have is the only Romanesque doorway. It is, however, not original to the tower.

The tower was restored in the 19th century, when the cap, roof, was rebuilt and the original door was restored. Otherwise, the tower remains largely original. Typical of round towers, the only door is set several feet off the ground, the tower only accessed by a ladder which would have been pulled up into the tower in times of trouble. Four openings at the top of the tower give 360-degree views around the countryside.

COUNTY LEITRIM

Creevelea Abbey and Friary—Creevelea Abbey, located on the outskirts of Dromahair (*Droim Dhá Thiar*) village, is a Franciscan Friary which was founded in 1508 on the banks of the River Bonet. It was in use until the 17th century when the Franciscans were forced to leave by the Cromwellian army. The nave, choir, tower and transept are well preserved, including a carving of St. Francis of Assisi preaching to the birds in the cloister. This site is now protected as a national monument.

Glencar Waterfall—Under the looming bulk of Ben Bulben, by the serene Glencar Lough, you can view the Glencar Falls, a spot haunted by the memory of William Butler Yeats. This beautiful waterfall, and the river leading up to it, has been modified for the tourist well enough. A walkway has been built and is maintained, as well as a visitor centre.

However, it is still relatively easy to find a quiet spot and contemplate the beauty of the surrounding countryside, the lough, and the waterfall. A farm near the entrance has several sheep and chickens to keep you amused, and the lough itself has reeds and breezes to soothe your soul. The lough is only about seven miles from Sligo Town, and while some of the roads are a bit narrow, it's a lovely drive through the trees.

'Where the wandering water gushes,
From the Hills above Glen-Car,
In pools among the rushes,
That scarce could bathe a star.'
- Yeats, The Stolen Child

Rose of Innisfree Boat Tour—Yeats country is full of places this famous poet referenced in his work, and this is no exception. This tour, boarded at the dock at Parke's Castle, will take you around Lough Gill and the island which was such inspiration for the Irish poet.

'I will arise and go now, and go to Innisfree,
and a small cabin build there, of clay and wattles made.'
- Yeats, The Isle of Innisfree

St. Hugh's Well and Cleighran More Sweat House—This well and stream is thought to have curative powers, and due to the high iron content from waters coming off the aptly named *Sliabh an Iarann*, Iron Mountain; the water is actually bright orange. The well is dedicated to St. Hugh, who lived in the 6th century. It is near the town of Cleighran More.

COUNTY LIMERICK

Castle Matrix—Near the south County Limerick town of Rathkeale, Castle Matrix was built in the 15th century by the Fitzgeralds. The name is possibly derived from 'Caisleán Matres'. The Matres were triple mother-goddesses of the pagan Celts, a type of pre-Christian Trinity. The castle has seen its own strife with the murder of James, the 9th Earl of Desmond by his tenants.

As well, Thomas Southwell rescued two hundred Palentine families from Germany and resettled them on the castle grounds in 1709. Further, this was the site where Sir Walter Raleigh met the poet Edmund Spencer, who was inspired to write 'The Faerie Queene.'

Raleigh was close friends with Edmund Southwell, Thomas' father, and visited the castle often. On one historic visit, Raleigh presented Edmund with a gift of some Virginia Tubers which were immediately planted on the castle lands. In 1610, the first crop of potatoes was harvested and distributed throughout the province.

By the 1960s, the castle had fallen into disrepair. As was typical during that decade, an American of Irish decent bought the castle and had it restored. It now contains a library with a collection of original documents pertaining to the Wild Geese. The O'Driscoll family maintains the castle and collection today.

Foynes Flying Boat Museum—Even though Foynes had a very short-lived history, 1939 to 1945, it was the primary terminus for the eastern route across the Atlantic. It was also the first route set up for passenger travel and holiday makers. Pan American World Airways', known as Pan Am, luxury flying boat, the Yankee Clipper, landed at Foynes in July 1939, and was the first commercial passenger flight between Europe and North America.

In the short seven years in which Foynes was the focal point for North Atlantic travel, Foynes saw many of the world's elite, from politicians and international businessmen to film stars, as well as active servicemen and wartime refugees. In 1942, Brendan O'Regan opened a restaurant and coffee shop in the Foynes Terminal and employed a chef called Joe Sheridan. It was Joe who realized that passengers who had come into the terminal from cold and rainy weather needed something to keep them warm and set about to make his special coffee, which became known as the Irish Coffee. The town of Foynes is easily accessed on the N69 south of Limerick City.

Lough Gur—(*Loch Gair*) On the road to Bruff, this lake forms a horseshoe shape and has many megalithic archeological sites around it, including Grange Stone Circle, which is the largest stone circle in Ireland. The stones are contiguous, touching each other, rather than standing alone around the circle. It has 113 stones and is 150 feet in diameter.

The circle is aligned with the rising sun on summer solstice. Also nearby is a dolmen, the remains of at least three crannogs are evident, and remains of Stone Age houses have been unearthed, the house outlines are known as 'The Spectacles.' A number of ring forts are found in the area, with one hill fort overlooking the lake. Some are Irish national monuments, the whole region a protected area.

There's a visitor centre with a picnic area near a very scenic spot on the shore. There is a castle near the entrance to the car park, Bourchier's Castle, named for Sir George Bourchier, the son of the second Earl of Bath, but it requires a bit of hiking to get up to it and is not open to the public.

Mussendun Temple, Derry

COUNTY (LONDON)DERRY

Bellaghy Bawn—Built around 1619 by Sir Baptist Jones, Bellaghy Bawn (*Baile Eachaidh* meaning 'Haughey's Townland'), is a fortified house and *bawn*, or defensive walls, located near Lough Beg. It is open to the public and has some exhibits on local natural history and poetry by the Nobel Laureate, Seamus Heaney.

Mussendun Temple—This stunning structure perches on the coast as part of the Downhill Demesne, a ruined estate towering over a sandy beach and a coastal railroad line. The temple used to be a library and commands an incredible view over the ocean. Don't miss exploring the extensive gardens and the manor house itself, as well as the small chapel further inland.

COUNTY LONGFORD

Abbeylara—(*Mainistir Leathrátha*, meaning 'Abbey of the Half Rath or Little Rath'), this is a village and ruin of a site which was said to have been founded in the 5th century by

St. Patrick. Today's village derives its name from a monastery, the great Abbey of Lerha, founded in 1205 by Hiberno-Norman magnate, Risteárd de Tiúit, for Cistercian monks. The monastery was dissolved in 1539, although its ruins are still apparent on approach to the village. An ancient earthen work, the Duncla (*Dún-chlaí*, meaning 'fortified ditch') or Black Pig's Dyke, which runs south-eastwards from Lough Gowna to Lough Kinale, goes through the larger parish of Abbeylara, and passes about one kilometer north of the village. The abbey ruins are very weathered and overgrown. Nearby are the only remains of stone circles in the Midlands, at Cloughernal, Cartronbore, and Clough.

Patrick's Motte—Granard Motte and Bailey is a very ancient structure that was supposedly erected some time before the Danish era, the time of the Vikings in Ireland 700-1169CE. A motte, not to be confused with a moat (a water-filled ditch at the bottom of a motte) is a flat-topped earthen mound, the top of which held a timber tower surrounded by a palisade.

Animals and soldiers were housed in the bailey, or courtyard. Richard de Tuite occupied it in 1199 as part of an initiative to extend Norman control over the region. This motte stands 534 feet above sea level and is reputedly the highest motte in Ireland. Stunning views from the summit include five lakes, parts of nine counties, and on the horizon, the outline of the Sliabh Bloom Mountains. Many myths surround this site, including one that says there is a castle concealed within the earthworks. Others say the motte holds vast treasures of gold. A statue of St. Patrick was erected on top of the Motte to mark in 1932.

COUNTY LOUTH

Mellifont Abbey—*An Mhainistir Mhór*, meaning 'the big abbey,' was the first Cistercian abbey built in Ireland. Founded in 1142 on the orders of Saint Malachy, Archbishop of Armagh,

Mellifont Abbey sits on the banks of the River Mattock near the town of Drogheda. By 1170, Mellifont had one hundred monks and three hundred lay brothers and became the model for other Cistercian abbeys built in Ireland. The abbey still bears its formal style of architecture imported from Cistercian abbeys in France.

Mellifont was the main abbey in Ireland until it was closed in 1539, when it became a fortified house. Mellifont Abbey is now a ruin, little of the original structure remains. Though you will find a 13th-century lavabo (where the monks washed their hands before eating), some Romanesque arches, and a 14th -century chapter house. There is an exhibit of medieval mason work, a garden centre, and a farm as well as a monastic guest house for a quiet retreat.

St. Mochta's House—St. Mochta is thought to be one of St. Patrick's disciples. There are no remains of St. Mochta's settlement. The ruined buildings at the site today are those of the 13th century church of St. Mary's Augustinian Priory and the stone-roofed oratory known as St. Mochta's House, which dates back to the late 12th century.

COUNTY MAYO

Achill's Abandoned Village—This is a village filled with abandoned cottages, gray bones baking in the sun. It is sobering to explore this large community, imagine those that used to occupy the houses, while seeing the modern whitewashed houses on the distant hillsides. Located at Slievemore, only the sheep still live in the 80 roofless stone homes. The cottages date from at least the 19th century and could be much older.

Ashleam Bay—Achill Island is very easy to get to, as there is a causeway built, so no ferry is necessary. It's not far from Westport, perhaps twenty miles northwest of the city. It is definitely worth a day trip to explore its infinite views! The Atlantic Drive meanders around the island, and there are many places to explore and find on this path. My favorite spot on the island is, hands down, Ashleam Bay. The bay has a sandy beach (Keem Strand), a rugged white cliff, from which you can witness the waves pounding in from the Atlantic and see the tiny houses dotting the hillsides.

There's a narrow switchback road to get up to the cliff top, but don't be worried, the buses can make it (we saw one while we were contemplating it) and if they can make it, so can you! The day we went, there were high winds, about 40-45 mph, and it was exhilarating to stand in this powerful force of nature. The sheep were less impressed by the fury, I think.

Bar in 'The Quiet Man, Cong, County Galway

Ceide Fields—This is a Neolithic site dedicated to the oldest known stone-walled fields in the world, approximately 6,000 years old. There is a visitor centre which helps to interpret the findings and it is fantastically situated on a sea cliff on the coast road to Belderrig.

Cong—One of the enduring legends of film history is the John Ford film, The Quiet Man, starring John Wayne and Maureen O'Hara. Set in rural Ireland in the early 20th century, many of the original film locations and buildings can be found around the village of Cong, such as Pat Cohan's Bar, the river and bridge, and the old, ruined church.

Alas, the cottage, White O' Morn, is lying in ruins, but plans are afoot to restore it to glory. There is a small museum to the film, in a thatched building around the corner from Pat Cohan's Bar. The Bar is restored, but don't try to go in just for a pic. The owners prefer if you buy a pint. Nearby is the impressive Ashford Castle, and much of the film was on the grounds of this grand estate.

Croagh Patrick—This is NOT a hidden place, but it is a very mystical place, and well worth a visit, even if you don't climb it. Nicknamed The Reek, this 764-meter mountain rises up near the town of Westport, dominating the skyline. It is a pilgrimage site on Reek Sunday, when thousands of pilgrims climb it, many in bare feet, to reach the small shrine to St. Patrick on the peak. The Saint supposedly fasted for 40 days on the summit and built a small church there in the 5th century.

Craogh Patrick, Mayo

Drive from Derrigimlagh to Dogs Bay—This lonely stretch of coastal road in Connemara is full of beauty, brash, and bold. It is rocky outcroppings, sandy beaches, and friendly ponies. Starting from Clifden, you follow the R341 down along the coast, and eventually make it to Roundstone.

Make sure to gas up first, as petrol stations are rare. You may want to pack a picnic lunch for the beach. The views along the road are stunning! There are a few commercial holiday cottages, and I recall a sign which advertised pony treks on the beaches, but other than this, this seems to be a mostly forgotten corner of the island.

Keep to the coastal road and explore the area. There are shades of the Burren here and there in the rocky landscape, but the fine sandy beach bottom belies the karstic landscape. Oh, and if you are into radio history, there is a site where the first transatlantic radio station was housed by Marconi, on the Derrigimlagh Bog. We spent a lovely morning driving along this road and ended up having lunch in Roundstone, a well-spent part of our day!

Famine Memorial—This stirring piece of sculpture by John Behan is called 'coffin ship', and it looks, from afar, like a bronze sculpture of one of the many tall ships which took the Irish from their homeland to the New World during the time of the Great Famine. However, as you get closer, it may chill you to realize the many figures on the boat are actually flowing skeletons, representative of the thousands and thousands who perished on ships stuffed with passengers, in horrible conditions.

Yet, they went, because the conditions back in Ireland were worse. It is a very sobering piece of art. I believe it is made more so by the fact it is in a lovely park, with a beautiful view of the bay. It makes the horror much more intense. Please, make some time to stop here while near Westport. Remember those who passed away to try to make a better life for themselves, their descendants, and their people. The memorial is about three miles from Westport, towards Croagh Patrick. Indeed, you can see the mountain behind it in many pictures.

The Highest Sea Cliffs in Europe—At a height of almost 700 meters, Croaghaun Mountain on Achill Island has the highest sea cliffs in Ireland and Great Britain, and arguably, in Europe. While you can drive to the car park at Keem Bay, you must then hike uphill from there, a journey well-rewarded with fantastic views over the Atlantic Ocean, unusual rock formations, and hidden mountain lakes. The area is home to some peregrine falcons; dolphins, porpoises, whales and basking sharks make their home in the nearby waters.

Kildavnet Castle—Kildavnet Castle, also called Carrick Kildavnet Castle is a simple 15th century tower copied Norman designs. The castle is about forty feet in height and has three levels, including a traditional vaulted ceiling. There is a finely preserved keep includes the remains of a boat slipway to one side. The tower's location was of strategic importance, situated at the mouth of Achill Sound, the passage that connects Clew Bay with Blacksod Bay.

While it's associated with the famous pirate queen, Grace O'Malley (*Granuaile* or *Grainne Mhaol*), the castle was most likely built by her ancestors in about 1429. There's no doubt that she did occupy this keep in her lifetime, as it was part of her holdings, though her main residence was at nearby Rockfleet Castle. Situated on a picturesque coastline near a small village, and just down the road from the stunning Keem Bay and Ashleam, this strong structure is literally RIGHT on the water, making this a definitely 'must see.'

Fourknocks Tomb, Meath

COUNTY MEATH

Hill of Tara—This is a site of ancient power, both spiritual and secular. For hundreds of years, the kings of Ireland were crowned here, and the earthworks and mounds speak of this ancient age. This is an especially good place if you can get there early, before the tour groups start. I went in 1996 and again in 2006, and it is a spectacular feeling to stand on top of the hill and see Ireland spread out before you like a patchwork quilt. It looks as if you can see the entire island from there. It is a humbling and beautiful experience.

Knowth/Dowth/Fourknocks—Living under the shadow of their grand cousin, Newgrange, the lesser-known passage tombs of Knowth, Dowth, and Fourknocks often get overlooked. However, they are unique and interesting, and well worth a visit. The tombs have carved kerbstones encircling it with various designs of megalithic art on them and have been dated to about 2,500 BCE. I first visited back in 1996, before the visitor centre required a tour to experience the tombs. Now, you must go through the *Brú na Bóinne* Visitor Centre in Donore, the same place you get Newgrange tours.

Loughcrew—Near the town of Oldcastle, this is a megalithic burial ground from about 3,500 BCE, near the Sliabh na Caillí (The Hag's Mountain). It is older and more accessible than nearby Newgrange. It has no visitor centre, and may have limited access, so please check before visiting. The legend is that the buildings were created when a giant hag, the Cailleach, strode across the land, dropping stones from her apron.

COUNTY MONAGHAN

Castleblayney—This Georgian manor house was once host to the Hope Diamond, and then became a convent before being abandoned. It was converted into a hotel at one point, but then closed after a fire caused considerable damage to the house. The grounds and lake are a lovely walk and exploration opportunity.

Castle Leslie—This is a thousand-acre estate and country house near the village of Glaslough in the Scottish Baronial style. There are gardens and a renaissance style cloister, three lakes, and a crannog on Dream Lake. The Leslie family is still in residence but have opened the estate to paying guests. There is a cookery school, a spa, a bar and restaurant, and riding trails.

COUNTY OFFALY

Charleville Castle—This is a neo-gothic architecture structure from the late 18th century and is home to a turbulent past. It has an impressive number of windows in the frontage, including a huge window over the front door, exquisite ceiling details, and perhaps even a ghost.

Clonmacnoise—This is not a hidden place, it's a major monastic site situated on the River Shannon. However, because it is rather inland and hidden away from the main tourist trail, I feel it needs to be pointed out as a spectacular place to visit. It has not one, but two round towers (one is crumbling). The site was established in the 6th century, and is extensive in ancient architecture, graves, and Celtic high crosses. Some artifacts have been relocated into the visitor centre to keep them from the elements, and replicas are placed outside.

Clonmacnoise, Offaly

COUNTY ROSCOMMON

Carrowcrory Cottage—This lovely place is dedicated to the mystical ways of Ireland. John Wilmot has built a garden with labyrinths, host afternoons of poetry and stories, music, and inner work. You can stay in the Lodge Farm or come by for a short visit. They are also a wealth of information of the sacred spaces in Ireland and have been kind enough to have contributed many suggestions I've included in this book.

Carrowmore, Sligo

Carrowmore Megaliths—Just about three miles north of Sligo, you can enter an ancient world of tombs, stone circles, and cairns. There are over 30 monuments in Carrowmore, all within about two square miles, with a nice visitor centre to help you understand the history of each. The monuments range from about 5,500 to 6,500 years old, and range from small, crumbling tombs to massive stone circles and cairns, such as Queen Maev's Cairn.

If you enjoy exploring megalithic sites, this is a must. Dedicate at least a couple hours to rambling among the stones and have decent walking shoes. While the OPW does a good job of maintaining the site, some of the grass and hills are a bit rough to walk on. There are a couple more circles on the other side of the road, so don't miss them! And say hello to the friendly horses in the next field.

Cave of the Cats—This is not a site for the faint of heart, it is a small cave entrance that is, legend says, the entrance to Hell. It has been a place of power for 6000 years. Also known as Oweynagat (Uaimh na gCat in Irish), it is associated with the Morrigan, Goddess of battle and strife, and is said to spew forth demonic creatures at Samhain (Hallowe'en). It is a small, unmarked wound on the side of a hill, almost obscured by greenery, and looks more like an animal's cave lair. If you do decide to try it, check in first at the Cruachan Aí Heritage Center at Tulsk.

COUNTY SLIGO

Caves of Keash/Keashcorran Mountain—also known as *Céis Coarran*, this area has seventeen caves under a mountain and an unopened cairn on the top. Lughnasa festivals were held on the mountain, and the place is associated with both Lugh and Cormac mac Airt, who was supposedly raised in the caves by a she-wolf.

Creevykeel Court Tomb—About 15 miles north of Sligo Town, there is a massive passage tomb dating about 6,000 years old called Creevykeel. It is RIGHT on the main road, and has a small car park to stop in. There is a clootie tree, or wish tree, at the entrance. You tie a ribbon or rag to the tree, and as the piece disintegrates, your wish is released into the world.

Please don't tie candy wrappers and plastic bags, I saw plenty of those on the tree. Besides, they won't disintegrate for DECADES. The tomb complex is quite large and consists of several 'courtyards' and passages between each. The passages are flanked by tall standing stones called orthostats. The site has been extensively restored and is worth at least an hour of exploration.

Deerpark Court Cairn—Many consider this to be the finest example of a central court tomb in Ireland. It sits on a ridge over Lough Gill and is surrounded by mountains. It has an oval shape about 50 feet long, with two galleries at the east end and one at the west.

Labby Rock—this is a rather amusing dolmen, as the capstone is covered in growth, making it look like it has a bushy head of hair. It's near the town of Carrickglass, and is named after the Irish word for bed, *leaba*.

Ben Bulben, Sligo

Lough Meelagh—This is a lake with several crannogs on man-made islands and dated from the early Christian period. Turlough O'Carolan, Ireland's last true bard, is buried nearby in the Kilronan graveyard. The site of Kilronan Castle has a structure called the Fairy House, a folly built for the castle. The Knockranny Wood on the shores is a wonderful place for a walk, and St. Lasair's Holy Well is worth a visit.

Strandhill seaweed baths—Who couldn't use a little pampering? Since Victorian times, spa baths in the west of Ireland offered some relaxation and tranquility. This tradition continues a few miles from Sligo town in Strandhill, where several companies offer full-service spa treatments with seaweed and mineral baths.

Ráth Cruachan—Known as Queen Maev's seat, the queen in the Ulster Cycle of Irish tales, this is a complex of archeological sites near the village of Tulsk and is the traditional capital of the ancient province of Connacht. It is the setting of several tales, such as the Táin Bó Cúailnge.

Drumcliffe, Sligo

COUNTY TIPPERARY

Ardmayle Castle—This is a ruin of a small tower house about four stories high, located about 5 km north of Cashel. It has stairs for climbing, but they are not for the timid. There is a vaulted loft, and a bit of a wild garden at the top levels. I wouldn't recommend testing the latrine hole, but there are secret chamber entrances and very scary stairways.

Cahir Castle—This impressive castle has been restored to medieval glory and is one of the finest medieval fortresses in Ireland. Built in the 12th century, it was the seat of the powerful Butler family for many centuries. It was also one of the few castles to escape destruction by Oliver Cromwell's armies. Its location on the River Suir made it ideal for use as a setting for the movie Excalibur. There is a great audio show in the little theater, and you can wander around on your own.

Celtic Plantarum—This Dundrum attraction has a rare collection of 60,000 plants, shrubs and trees with eight acres, and two miles of pathways through them. It has a range of reconstructed follies and field monuments, making the journey sort of like a concentrated trip through the formal gardens of Ireland.

The Craft Granary—If you want to do some local shopping, make a visit to this lovingly restored grain store, which showcases local handcrafted items from the area. It has cards, photos, woodcrafts, glassware, and all sorts of exquisite gifts—none of the typical touristy tat that many gift stores have all too much of. It is down the street from Castle Cahir, towards the center of town.

Cahir Castle, Tipperary

Nenagh Castle—In the town of Nenagh, this castle is a well-preserved round Norman tower keep, built around 1200 CE. It was still held by the Butler family until 1997, when the last owner died without a male heir. The views from the top of the recently opened tower are commanding, and the crenellations and windows at the top make it charming and quite picturesque.

St. Berrihert's Kyle and Well—The kyle and well are well hidden in the Galtee Mountains. It is an adventure, but if you persist, it is well worth exploring. There are seventy-two early medieval inscribed stone slabs, and the kyle is a large oval enclosure with a bank of stones and earth.

Some of the slabs and crosses date from the 7th century and was thought to be the site of an early church founded by St. Berrihert, a Saxon cleric. There is a clootie tree for tying wishes, a small sacred spring, and a bullaun stone for collecting water, which is said to imbue healing powers.

Shanballyedmond Court Cairn—This court tomb near the village of Rear Cross is a two-chambered gallery and runs about 5 meters long. It has a horseshoe-shaped structure and is situated on a hill high enough to see the hills surrounding the area. It is not difficult to get to as it's in a residential area, and there is a car park nearby.

Swiss Cottage—This is a charming, almost over-charming, Victorian cottage built by the Butler family of Cahir Castle to use as a place to entertain guests. The building style is cottage orné, a type of ornamental folly. Everything about the cottage architecture is derived from nature, from the spiderweb design in the entry hall to the hand-painted green ivy wallpaper and matching china. It is like something out of a fairy tale, with a thatched roof, stone steps, and a long, picturesque walk from the castle to the cottage along the River Suir. It has an extensive guided tour inside the house, and plenty of places to wander outside. Enjoy yourself in this Victorian retreat.

COUNTY TYRONE

Beaghmore Stone Circles—(*Bheitheach Mhór*) This is a complex of seven stone circles on the Sperrin Mountains, near the town of Cookstown. There are stone rows, cairns, and pairs of standing stones. The stones are small, and only a few are more than a half meter in height.

Donaghmore High Cross—They monastery at Donaghmore was founded by St. Patrick in the 6th century and houses an impressive high cross. The cross has carved scenes on both sides, including the Annunciation to the shepherds, the Adoration of the Magi, and several others, including the Crucifixion. While it is badly weathered, it is very impressive for its height (4.8 meters) and carvings. There is a replica in the nearby cemetery that shows how the carvings may have looked when new.

Connemara Pony

President Grant's ancestral home—For those with an interest in US history, a visit to President Grant's ancestral home might be of interest. It has been restored to that of a typical 19th century cottage, with a turf fire and outhouses. Admission is free to the Simpson farm (Simpson is the S in Ulysses S. Grant), and it has been restored to look as it did in the 19th century. It is close to the town of Ballygawley.

St. Patrick's Chair—This is a rock construction, also known as the Druid's Chair and Well, or St. Brigid's Well. It is off the Ulster Way footpath and within Altadeven Wood. The chair is a huge stone block shaped like a chair or throne. The well is filled with natural water and is reputed to have healing powers.

Wellbrook Beetling Mill—Beetling was a step in the production of linen, and this mill still holds the original machinery from the late 18th century. There is a wheel, sluice gate, and traditional cottage in a lovely, idyllic setting. It was the last working beetling mill in Northern Ireland, located in Cookstown, and has on-hands demonstrations of the linen.

COUNTY WATERFORD

Dromana Gate—This Hindu Gothic gate in Cappoquin, on the road to Villerstown, was built early in the 19th century, and is unique. The original building was made from wood and papier-mâché, for the owner and his wife, and they loved it so much, they rebuilt it in stone.

King John's Castle (aka Dungarvan Castle)—Located in the heart of Dungarvan, this castle is a polygonal shell keep with a curtain wall, and it dates to the 12th century. This is more common to England than Ireland. The keep includes a military barracks which are restored and open to visitors with an explanatory exhibition.

COUNTY WESTMEATH

Tullynally Castle Gardens, Westmeath

Beehive Tomb—This tomb, built by Adolphus Cooke for his father, was meant to reincarnate the deceased into a bee, complete with a hole in the top so he can fly out. Cooke himself evidently dug foxholes, thinking he would be reincarnated as a fox. It is located within the grounds of St. John the Baptist's Church in the townland of Reynella.

Tullynally Castle—This fantastic Gothic country house has woodland gardens, a limestone grotto, ornamental lakes, and even a Tibetan waterfall garden. Also known as Pakenham Hll, it was built in the 17th century.

Hill of Uisneach—Historically, the Hill of Uisneach was the seat of the high kings of Ireland, along with the Hill of Tara, which probably superseded the honor. It is located between the villages of Ballymore and Loughanavally, just west of Mullingar, and is considered the geographic center, or 'mythical naval' of the island.

There have been ceremonies and rituals performed there back through the ancient tales and stories. Around the hill are many places with spiritual connections, such as barrows, cairns, a holy well, and ancient roads. It is also considered the place where the goddess Eriú met Amergin the Bard when the Milesians came to Ireland.

The Jealous Wall—This was a large folly, or 'sham ruin', built on the Belvedere House grounds by Earl Robert Rochfort. It is located between Lough Ennell and Mullingar Golf Club. He built this, the largest folly in Ireland, when his brother built a large house next door, so he wouldn't have to see it. There are several gardens, homes, and other follies on the grounds of the House.

Kilbeggan Distillery—Kilbeggan is a small pot still distillery on the River Brosna and offers both regular tours and VIP tours. The VIP tour will give you a closer look at the process and a personal tour guide. You can even go home with a bottle of whiskey and a personalized label, if you like.

COUNTY WEXFORD

Blackwater Village Grotto—If you like finding hidden holy wells, here is one hidden near Blackwater Village. There is a thatched cottage, a stone bridge, river and waterfall, and a Marian shrine. There is a procession from St. Brigid's Church every year during the feast of Corpus Christi.

Hook Head—While lighthouses are typically dramatically situated, the Hook lighthouse is also one of the oldest in the world, and the oldest operating lighthouse in Ireland. It was founded by Welsh monk St. Dubhain in the 5th century, though at the time it was merely a bonfire. The Normans built a more permanent structure in the 13th century, and monks manned the lighthouse with peat and wood fires for centuries. There is a nearby castle called Crook Castle, which may have inspired the phrase 'By Hook or By Crook.'

Tintern Abbey—On Bannow Bay, this is a Cistercian monastery which passed through many hands, each one leaving its mark in architecture and structure. It was built by William Marshal around 1200 CE, as legend has it, as a result of a vow he made when his boat was caught in a storm. As a result, it is sometimes known as 'Tintern de Voto', or 'Tintern of the Vow'. William Marshall also founded the town of New Ross, which is famous for the Ros Tapestry, Ireland's equivalent of the Bayeux Tapestry. The Abbey was styled after Tintern Abbey in Wales and is now a partially restored ruin.

COUNTY WICKLOW

Glendalough—Glendalough means the Glen of Two Lakes, and it is a delightful place. It has an extensive monastery, round tower, visitor centre, all in a beautiful, peaceful valley. The biggest problem is that everyone knows it, and it is frequently overrun with busloads of tourists, masking the quiet serenity of the site. The solution is to arrive early or late, when most of the other visitors aren't there. When you do, you can drink in the spirituality of the place and setting. Venture off to the Upper Lake, explore to find the Reefert Church, St. Kevin's Cell, *Teampall-na-Skellig*, and St. Kevin's Bed.

Powerscourt Falls, Estate and Gardens—Nestled near Great Sugar Loaf Mountain, this lovely spot is often cited as the highest waterfall in Ireland at a height of 400 feet. There are rocks at the bottom to climb upon, and a playground for the children. It is near the Powerscourt Estate, which is also worth some exploration. Only a portion of the house is open for visitors as it was damaged by fire in 1974 and partially renovated in 1996, but the gardens are the largest gardens in Ireland and a must see.

Wander through the Japanese Garden, Italianate Garden, Rose Garden, and Herb Garden. Climb the Pepperpot Tower, stroll along Rhododendron Walk (stunningly beautiful when in bloom in June), find the Dolphin Pond and Pet Cemetery, and view the largest pond on the estate, Trinton Pond, from the famous Perron, and many more areas in the luscious backdrop of the imposing house. Episodes of the TV series, The Tudors, and a scene in the film Excalibur were filmed around the gardens and waterfall.

Wicklow Mountains—This is another of those 'too big to be hidden' places, but often it is missed by those charmed by Dublin and the more specific sites. There are walking trails and lots of places to enjoy nature with climbing, hunting, fishing, and picnics, but even just driving through this park on one of the lonely, winding roads is worth dedicating some time and wonder. It is designated as a National Park, and has many particular sites worth exploring, such as Glenmacness Waterfall (near Laragh), the hill forts and abbey near Baltinglass, and Glendalough lakes and Monastery.

Dunluce Castle, Antrim

Conclusion

I hope your journey through this book brought you delight, knowledge, and a passion for the magic and mystery which is my soul's home, Ireland. I do believe places we go, things we see, can be enriched by background knowledge in myth, history, and a sense of place. My purpose in writing this book was to share this background with others, and perhaps infect them with my sense of wonder at the Emerald Isle.

Truly, any place is magical with the right frame of mind and the right attitude when visiting. However, I think Ireland holds a special bit of magic of its very own, secure in the mystery of history and the wealth of historical sites, beautiful gardens, hidden wells, and megalithic monuments. It is a place to hold dear in our hearts, whether we visit for a few days or a few years. Some of us lose our hearts forever in the emerald hills and hidden hollows, looking for the Sídhe and dark riders in the night.

I am one of those people, and some day, I will move to my beloved soul's home.

When the magical secrets of The Emerald Isle beckon, will she survive answering the call?

Can Valentia embrace her elusive legacy while protecting those she loves?

Start reading **Legacy of Hunger** to trace a family treasure today!

Thank You!

Thank you so much for enjoying this guide. If you've enjoyed the story, please consider leaving a review so other readers can discover Ireland's magic!

If you would like to get updates, sneak previews, sales, and **FREE STUFF**, please sign up for my newsletter.

See all the books available through Green Dragon Publishing:
http://www.greendragonartist.com/books

Maps and Resources

ONLINE RESOURCES

General Ireland Information

Discover Ireland—http://www.discoverireland.ie.
Irish Pubs—http://irishpubs.com.
Green Dragon Artist—https://greendragonartist.com/travel—my own website dedicated to my books, art, and trip reports.
Ireland Expert—http://www.irelandexpert.com—Pat Preston offers great advice. She has passed away, but her excellent advice is still online.
Ireland Travel Kit—http://www.irelandtravelkit.com—filled with hidden gems and fairs.
Ireland Yes—http://www.IrelandYes.com—Michele Erdvig has been to Ireland over 50 times, has a helpful forum, and a fantastic book.
Irish Central—http://www.irishcentral.com—news for Irish and Irish Americans.
Irish Fireside—http://www.irishfireside.com—great blog and podcast on Irish travel.
My Guide Ireland—http://www.myguideireland.com.
RTE—Raidío na Gaeltachta—http://www.rte.ie—listen live to Irish radio.
Visit Britain—http://www.visitbritain.com—for those venturing to the Northern Ireland.

Mythical, Mystical, Historical or Hidden Places

Antrim Rambler—https://www.youtube.com/channel/UC0MU1FBRDt7N5yslEBvN3pg—for guided walks.
Celtic Myth Podshow—https://podcasts.apple.com/us/podcast/celtic-myth-podshow/id272848127—dramatizations of Celtic myths.

Celtic Ways—http://www.celticways.com- a lovely place in west Ireland with a spiritual maze and farm.
Craggaunowen—https://www.craggaunowen.ie.
Irish History Podcasts—http://irishhistorypodcast.ie—a great resource for Irish history.
Irish Pagan School—https://irishpaganschool.com – reliable information on Irish Paganism.
Megalithic Ireland—http://www.megalithicireland.com/—megalithic sites in Ireland.
Powerful Places—http://www.powerfulplaces.com—a great set of books and a blog for spiritual places in the British Isles.
Sacred Texts—http://www.sacred-texts.com—a guide to tales from William Yeats, Lady Gregory and many others.
Stone Pages—http://www.stonepages.com—a guide to stone circles and standing stones.
Story Archaeology—https://storyarchaeology.com—a podcast exploring the Irish myths.
Thin Place—http://www.thinplace.net—a guide to spiritual places.
UNESCO World Heritage Centre—http://whc.unesco.org—listing of World Heritage sites.

Travel Related Sites

Aer Lingus—http://www.aerlingus.com.
Aran Island Ferries—http://www.aranislandferries.com—for travel to the Aran Islands.
Ashford Castle—http://www.ashford.ie.
Auto Europe—http://www.autoeurope.com—Car Rental.
Bus Eireann—http://www.buseireann.ie.
Conn's Ireland Car Rental—https://www.connsireland.com.
Dan Dooley—http://www.dan-dooley.ie—Car Rental.
Enterprise Car Rental—http://www.enterprise.com.
Expedia—http://www.expedia.com.
Fodor's Forums—http://www.fodors.com/community—great help (and some snarky advice) from others who have been there.
Green Traveller—http://www.greentraveller.co.uk—for planning ecoholidays.
Insure My Trip—http://www.insuremytrip.com—to compare travel insurance plans.
Ireland Hostels—http://www.hostels-ireland.com.
Irish Rail—http://www.irishrail.ie—Train Timetables.
Ireland with Kids—http://irelandwithkids.com.
Seat Guru—http://www.seatguru.com—find out which airline seats are best.
Self-Catering Rentals—http://www.selfcatering-ireland.com.
Trip Advisor—www.tripadvisor.com—for researching the B&Bs, hotels, and sites.
Unique Irish Hostels—http://www.uniqueirishhostels.com.
Via Michelin—http://www.viamichelin.com—great for planning routes and times.

Discount Sources

Airfare Watchdog—http://www.airfarewatchdog.com—for discount airfare.
Dublin Pass—http://www.dublinpass.ie.
Dublin Sightseeing Tours—http://www.dublinsightseeing.ie/citytour.aspx.
Flyertalk—http://www.flyertalk.com—for those who travel frequently.
Heritage Card—http://www.heritageireland.ie.
Kayak—http://www.kayak.com.

Last Minute Travel—http://www.lastminutetravel.com—for last minute airfare deals.
Lonely Planet—http://www.lonelyplanet.com—good all-around site, especially for tight budgets.
STA Travel—http://www.statravel.com—for student and teacher travel.
Student Universe—http://www.studentuniverse.com—for student and teacher travel.
Travel Zoo—http://www.travelzoo.com—for discount airfare.
Veteran's Advantage—http://www.veteransadvantage.com—for veteran travel.

Photography Sources

DP Review—http://www.dpreview.com—to compare cameras.
Lulu—http://www.lulu.com—for book and calendar printing.
Simply Canvas—http://www.simplycanvas.com—for photographic printing.
White House Custom Copies—http://www.whcc.com—for photographic printing.

PRINT RESOURCES

Foster, RF . *The Oxford Illustrated History of Ireland.* Oxford: Oxford University Press, 1989.
Mac Eachaidh, Seán. *A Guide to the Silence of the Irish Other World.* Seán Mac Eachaidh BA, 2012.
Matthews, John. *Celtic Myths and Legends*, Pitkin Guides, 2001.
Moody, T.W; Martin, F.X; Byrne, F.J, eds. *A New History of Ireland VIII: A Chronology of Irish History to 1976—A Companion to Irish History Part I.* Oxford Clarendon Press, 1982.
O'Rahilly, Thomas Francis. *Early Irish history and mythology*. Dublin, 1946.
Sjoestedt, Marie-Louise. *Gods and Heroes of the Celts*. London, 1949. Translation by Miles Dillon of Sjoestedt's *Dieux et héros des Celtes*. Paris, 1940.
Stewart, R.J. *Celtic Gods, Celtic Goddesses*. London, 1992.

Thoor Ballylee, Galway

Appendix

Irish (pronunciation guide)—English name and definition

Ailill mac Máta (ahLEEL mak MAHta)—a king of Connacht.
Adomnán (AH-dom-nawn)—a monk of Iona, follower of Columba.
Amergin (AHM-er-gin)—the bard of the Mílesians.
An Mhainistir Mhór (an VAH-een-ish-teer vor).
Annach an Phuic (AN-nakh an FOO-ick).
Aoife (EE-fah)—daughter of Dermot MacMurrough and wife of Richard de Clare, 'Strongbow'.
Baile Eachaidh (BWA-leh EEKH-eye)—Bellaghy, meaning 'Haughey's Townland', a village in Londonderry, Northern Ireland.
Balor (BAY-lor) of the Evil Eye—a king of the Fomóire.
Bán (Bawn)—white.
Banba (BAHN-ba)—one of three sisters of the Tuatha dé Danaan.
Bean Sídhe (BAN-shee)—a female fairy, specifically one who wails at a person's death.
Bheitheach Mhór (VAY-thee-akh vor)—Beaghmore, a megalithic site in County Tyrone.
Bodhrán (BOW-rahn)—an Irish drum.
Bres (BRESH)—a half Tuatha/half Fomóir prince.
Brian Bóruma mac Cennétig (BREE-an BOR-oom-ah mak KEN-eh-teeg)/Brian Boru of Kennedy—a High King of Ireland.
Brigid or Brid (BREE-jid or BREED)—Brigit, A goddess or saint of Ireland.
Brocca (BROKE-ah)—Brigit's mother.
Cáilléach (KAHL-ee-akh)—Calleach, or Hag, a goddess who brings the winter.
Cailléach Bheara (KAHL-ee-ack VER-ah)—The Hag of Beara, a peninsula of southwestern Ireland.
Carraig an Phoill (KAR-ag an FOE-il)—Carrigafoyle—a castle in County Kerry.
Céili (KAY-lee)—a party.
Cessair (CHESS-air)—leader of the first inhabitants of Ireland, Noah's granddaughter.
Cipín (CHIP-een)—a small stick used to beat the bodhrán.
Clochán (KLOE-khawn)—a dry stone hut with a corbelled roof.
Cluricaun (KLUR-i-kawn)—an Irish fairy.
Colm Cille (KOL-um khill)—St. Columba, 'Dove of the Church', who brought Christianity to Scotland from Ireland.
Conchobar (KAHN-ko-bar)—a king of Ulster.
Conn of the Hundred Battles (KAHN)—a high king of Ireland.
Connla (KAHN-lah)—son of Cú Chulainn.
Cormac mac Airt (KOR-mac mak ayrt)—a king of Ireland, known for his wise judgments.

Cromlech Cathair Croagh Deag (KROM-lekh KA-hayr KROH-ah jyeg)—an ancient settlement called 'An Shrone' or 'The City'.
Cromm Crúaich (krom KROO-ahkh)—a Celtic god associated with human sacrifice.
Cú (KOO)—hound.
Cú Chulainn (KOO khoo-lann)/Cuchulain—a hero, son of Lugh and Deichtine (DEEKH-tee-neh), originally named Sétanta (say-TAHN-tah).
Cúlann (KHOO-lann)—a smith whose hound is killed by Sétanta.
Dagda (DAG-dah)—a Celtic god, known as the 'good' god, a father god.
Dal Cais (dahl KAYSH)—a ruling tribe of Thomond.
Danú (DAH-noo)—a Celtic goddess, the mother goddess.
Dara mac Fachtna (DAH-rah mak FAHKHT-nah)—an Ulster chieftain in the Cattle Raid of Cooley.
Deichtine (JYEKH-tee-neh)—sister of Conchobar, mother of Sétanta.
Deirdre (DEER-dreh)—Conchobar's bride-to-be.
Diarmait mac Murchada (dee-AYR-met mak mur-KHA-dah)—Dermot MacMurrough—a king of Leinster.
Droim Dhá Thiar (DROH-im zha HEE-ar)—Dromahair Village.
Dubh Linn (DOOV lin)—Black Pool, which became Dublin.
Dubhthach (DOOV-hakh)—a pagan chieftain of Ireland, father of Brigid.
Dullahan (DOO-lah-han)—a fairy, a headless rider.
Dún Ailinne (doon AY-lin-eh)—Dun Aulin—a ceremonial site in County Kildare.
Dún Aonghasa (doon ang-OH-sah)—Dun Aengus—a prehistoric fort on Inis Mor.
Dún Másc (doon MAHSK)—the Rock of Dunamase—a 9th century fort in County Laois.
Dún-chlaí (doon KHLAY)—duncla, a fortified ditch.
Emain Macha (EH-mayn MAKH-a)—the royal seat of Ulster.
Eóghanachta (YO-ghan-ack-tah)/Eugenians—a ruling tribe of Desmond.
Eriú (EY-ree-oo)—one of three sisters of the Tuatha dé Danaan.
Feadóg (FAY-dog)—an Irish tin whistle.
Fionn mac Cumhaill (FINN mack KOOWOL)/Finn MacCool—the leader of the Fianna, guardians of Ireland.
Fintan mac Bochra (FINN-tan mak BOW-khra)—a seer who accompanied Cessair to Ireland.
Fir Bolg (FEER bolg)—A race of people, possibly giants.
Fodla (FOD-lah)—one of three sisters of the Tuatha dé Danaan.
Fomóire (fo-MOR-eh) /Fomórians—a race of seafarers.
Fulacht Fiadh (FOO-lakht FEE-ath)—a cooking pit.
Gáilióin (GAY-lee-oyn)—one of the three tribes of Fir Bolg.
Gea bolg (GAY-a bolg)—a magical spear.
Geis (GAY-iss)—a curse or obligation.
Gleann Cholm Cille (GLEN kholm kill)—Glencolmcille, the birthplace of St. Columba.
Granuile/Grainne Mhaol (GRAN-weel-eh/GRAN-ye VAY-ol)—Grace O'Malley, a 16th century pirate queen.
Grianán Ailigh (GREE-an-an AY-lee)—Grianan of Aileach, a stone ring fort in County Donegal.
Grogoch (GROW-gokh)—a half-fairy, half-human entity.
Guagán Barra (GOW-gahn BAR-rah)—Gougane Barra, or the Rock of Barra, a monastery and settlement in County Cork.
Íth (EETH)—a Mílesian, nephew of Míl.

Labraid Loingsech (LAH-brayd LONG-shekh)—a King of Ireland.

Laeghaire (LEE-hayr)—a king of Ireland, possibly converted by St. Patrick.

Leabhar na h-Uidhri (LOW-ar nah HWEE-three)—the Book of the Dun Cow—one of the oldest surviving Irish literature manuscripts.

Leac na Scail (LAC nah scayl)—Kilmogue dolmen.

Leipreachán (LEP-reh-kawn)—Leprechaun, a fairy taking the form of an old man, a cobbler.

Loch Gair (LOCK gayr)—Lough Gur, a lake in County Limerick.

Lú/Lugh (LOO)—A man of the Tuatha dé Danann, noted for his many gifts.

Lúnasadh (LOO-nah-sah)—Lunasa, the month of August in Irish, also the name of an Irish musical group.

Máel Mórda mac Murchada (mayl MOR-dah mak mur-KHA-dah)—An Irish king, the enemy of Brian Boru.

Mainistir Leathrátha (MAYN-ish-teer LEEH-raw-ha)—Abbey of the Half Rath, in County Longford.

Manannán mac Lír (mah-NAN-an mak leer)—Irish sea god

Medb/Maev (MAYV)—a queen of Connacht.

Míl—(MEEL)—a Celtic chieftain from the north of Spain.

Mílesians (mil-EE-zhins)—Celtic tribe from the north of Spain, who invaded Ireland.

Mo anam an bhaile (mo AN-am an VWAHL-eh)—my soul's home.

Morrigan (MOR-i-gahn)—a goddess of war, fertility and horses.

Murúch (MOOR-ookh)—merrow, a mermaid or merman.

Myrddin (MEER-thin)—the Welsh name of Merlin.

Na Seacht dTeampaill (nah shokht TEM-pill)—the Seven Churches, a ruined temple site on Inis Mór.

Neimheadh (NEH-ved)—Nemed, the leader of the third group of invaders to Ireland.

Niall of the Nine Hostages (NEEL)—a leader of the O'Neill clan.

Noísi (NOY-shee)—Deirdre's husband.

Nuadha Airgetlámh (noo-AH-tha AYR-get-lav)—Nuada of the Silver Arm, the first king of the Tuatha dé Danaan.

Oisín (OY-shin)—Ossian, an Irish poet, a member of the Fianna, and son of Fionn mac Cumhaill.

Partholón (PAR-thol-ahn)—the leader of the second group of invaders to Ireland.

Poítin (po-CHEEN)—Potcheen, an Irish moonshine.

Púca (POO-kah)—Pookha, an Irish ghost horse.

Raidió na Gaeltachta (RAY-dee-oh nah GAYL-tack-tah)—the Gaelic language radio station.

Ráth Cruachan (rath KROO-ah-kahn)—Rathcroghan, an archeological site in County Roscommon.

Fianna (fee-AN-ah)—the Red Branch, the warriors of Finn McCool.

Sadhbh (SATHV)—Saba, the mother of Oisín by Fionn mac Cumhaill.

Scáthach (SKATH-ack)—a warrior woman who runs a school on the Isle of Skye.

Sceilig Mhichíl (SKAY-lig VEE-khil)—Skellig Michael—a group of islands in County Kerry.

Sceilig Mhór (SKAY-lig VOR)—the largest island in Skellig Michael.

Seanchaí (SAN-eh-khay)—shanachie, an Irish storyteller or historian.

Sean-nós (SHAWN-nose)—a traditional style of Irish song.

Seisiún (SESH-oon)—session, a traditional Irish music jam.

Sétanta (se-TAWN-tah)—the birth name of Cú Chulainn.
Sí Bheag, Sí Mhór (shee beg, shee more)—Little Hill, Big Hill, a traditional Irish tune by Turlough O'Carolan.
Sídhe (SHEE)—another name for the Tuatha dé Danann.
Sliabh na Caillí (SLEEV nah KAY-lee)—Slieve na Cailliagh, the Hag's Mountain, in County Meath.
Suidhne (SWEED-nah)—a pagan king.
Tain Bó Cuailnge (tawn bow KOOL-ng-eh)—The Cattle Raid of Cooley, a legendary tale from early Irish literature.
Tuan mac Cairill (TOO-awn mak KAY-rill)—a follower of Partholón.
Tuatha dé Danann (TOO-a-ha day DAh-nin)—a magical race.
Uí Néill (WE NEEL)/O'Neill—a ruling tribe of Connacht and Ulster.
Uilleann (YOO-linn)—Elbow pipes, the Irish form of bagpipes.
Uisce Beatha (ISH-kee BAH-ha)—Whiskey, the Water of Life.
Uisnech (ISH-nekh)—Ushnagh, an ancient ceremonial site in County Westmeath.

Sliabh Liag Cliffs, Donegal

Dedication

I would like to dedicate this book to my parents, D. Paul and Judy. My love of art and travel, as well as my sense of determination comes directly from them, and I love them deeply for it. Also, I would like to thank my supportive husband, Jason, without whom I would be lost and adrift.

About the Author

Christy Nicholas writes under several pen names, including Rowan Dillon, CN Jackson, and Emeline Rhys. She's an author, artist, and accountant. After she failed to become an airline pilot, she quit her ceaseless pursuit of careers that began with the letter 'A' and decided to concentrate on her writing. Since she has Project Completion Compulsion, she is one of the few authors with no unfinished novels.

Christy has her hands in many crafts, including digital art, beaded jewelry, writing, and photography. In real life, she's a CPA, but having grown up with art all around her (her mother, grandmother, and great-grandmother are/were all artists), it sort of infected her, as it were. She wants to expose the incredible beauty in this world, hidden beneath the everyday grime of familiarity and habit, and share it with others. She uses characters out of time and places infused with magic and myth, writing magical realism stories in both historical fantasy and time travel flavors.

Social Media Links:

Blog: www.GreenDragonArtist.net
Website: www.GreenDragonArtist.com
Facebook: www.facebook.com/greendragonauthor
Instagram: www.instagram.com/greendragonartist9
TikTok: www.tiktok.com/@greendragonauthor

Made in the USA
Coppell, TX
09 November 2024